D1597437

SSAT Lower Level Prep Book

Elementary Level SSAT Prep Book Team

Copyright © 2017 Elementary Level SSAT Prep Book Team

All rights reserved.

FREE Test Taking Tips DVD Offer

To help us better serve you, we have developed a Test Taking Tips DVD that we would like to give you for FREE. **This DVD covers world-class test taking tips that you can use to be even more successful when you are taking your test.**

All that we ask is that you email us your feedback about your study guide. Please let us know what you thought about it – whether that is good, bad or indifferent.

To get your **FREE Test Taking Tips DVD**, email freedvd@studyguideteam.com with "FREE DVD" in the subject line and the following information in the body of the email:

> a. The title of your study guide.
>
> b. Your product rating on a scale of 1-5, with 5 being the highest rating.
>
> c. Your feedback about the study guide. What did you think of it?
>
> d. Your full name and shipping address to send your free DVD.

If you have any questions or concerns, please don't hesitate to contact us at freedvd@studyguideteam.com.

Thanks again!

Table of Contents

Quick Overview

As you draw closer to taking your exam, effective preparation becomes more and more important. Thankfully, you have this study guide to help you get ready. Use this guide to help keep your studying on track and refer to it often.

This study guide contains several key sections that will help you be successful on your exam. The guide contains tips for what you should do the night before and the day of the test. Also included are test-taking tips. Knowing the right information is not always enough. Many well-prepared test takers struggle with exams. These tips will help equip you to accurately read, assess, and answer test questions.

A large part of the guide is devoted to showing you what content to expect on the exam and to helping you better understand that content. Near the end of this guide is a practice test so that you can see how well you have grasped the content. Then, answer explanations are provided so that you can understand why you missed certain questions.

Don't try to cram the night before you take your exam. This is not a wise strategy for a few reasons. First, your retention of the information will be low. Your time would be better used by reviewing information you already know rather than trying to learn a lot of new information. Second, you will likely become stressed as you try to gain a large amount of knowledge in a short amount of time. Third, you will be depriving yourself of sleep. So be sure to go to bed at a reasonable time the night before. Being well-rested helps you focus and remain calm.

Be sure to eat a substantial breakfast the morning of the exam. If you are taking the exam in the afternoon, be sure to have a good lunch as well. Being hungry is distracting and can make it difficult to focus. You have hopefully spent lots of time preparing for the exam. Don't let an empty stomach get in the way of success!

When travelling to the testing center, leave earlier than needed. That way, you have a buffer in case you experience any delays. This will help you remain calm and will keep you from missing your appointment time at the testing center.

Be sure to pace yourself during the exam. Don't try to rush through the exam. There is no need to risk performing poorly on the exam just so you can leave the testing center early. Allow yourself to use all of the allotted time if needed.

Remain positive while taking the exam even if you feel like you are performing poorly. Thinking about the content you should have mastered will not help you perform better on the exam.

Once the exam is complete, take some time to relax. Even if you feel that you need to take the exam again, you will be well served by some down time before you begin studying again. It's often easier to convince yourself to study if you know that it will come with a reward!

Test-Taking Strategies

1. Predicting the Answer

When you feel confident in your preparation for a multiple-choice test, try predicting the answer before reading the answer choices. This is especially useful on questions that test objective factual knowledge or that ask you to fill in a blank. By predicting the answer before reading the available choices, you eliminate the possibility that you will be distracted or led astray by an incorrect answer choice. You will feel more confident in your selection if you read the question, predict the answer, and then find your prediction among the answer choices. After using this strategy, be sure to still read all of the answer choices carefully and completely. If you feel unprepared, you should not attempt to predict the answers. This would be a waste of time and an opportunity for your mind to wander in the wrong direction.

2. Reading the Whole Question

Too often, test takers scan a multiple-choice question, recognize a few familiar words, and immediately jump to the answer choices. Test authors are aware of this common impatience, and they will sometimes prey upon it. For instance, a test author might subtly turn the question into a negative, or he or she might redirect the focus of the question right at the end. The only way to avoid falling into these traps is to read the entirety of the question carefully before reading the answer choices.

3. Looking for Wrong Answers

Long and complicated multiple-choice questions can be intimidating. One way to simplify a difficult multiple-choice question is to eliminate all of the answer choices that are clearly wrong. In most sets of answers, there will be at least one selection that can be dismissed right away. If the test is administered on paper, the test taker could draw a line through it to indicate that it may be ignored; otherwise, the test taker will have to perform this operation mentally or on scratch paper. In either case, once the obviously incorrect answers have been eliminated, the remaining choices may be considered. Sometimes identifying the clearly wrong answers will give the test taker some information about the correct answer. For instance, if one of the remaining answer choices is a direct opposite of one of the eliminated answer choices, it may well be the correct answer. The opposite of obviously wrong is obviously right! Of course, this is not always the case. Some answers are obviously incorrect simply because they are irrelevant to the question being asked. Still, identifying and eliminating some incorrect answer choices is a good way to simplify a multiple-choice question.

4. Don't Overanalyze

Anxious test takers often overanalyze questions. When you are nervous, your brain will often run wild, causing you to make associations and discover clues that don't actually exist. If you feel that this may be a problem for you, do whatever you can to slow down during the test. Try taking a deep breath or counting to ten. As you read and consider the question, restrict yourself to the particular words used by the author. Avoid thought tangents about what the author *really* meant, or what he or she was *trying* to say. The only things that matter on a multiple-choice test are the words that are actually in the question. You must avoid reading too much into a multiple-choice question, or supposing that the writer meant something other than what he or she wrote.

5. No Need for Panic

It is wise to learn as many strategies as possible before taking a multiple-choice test, but it is likely that you will come across a few questions for which you simply don't know the answer. In this situation, avoid panicking. Because most multiple-choice tests include dozens of questions, the relative value of a single wrong answer is small. Moreover, your failure on one question has no effect on your success elsewhere on the test. As much as possible, you should compartmentalize each question on a multiple-choice test. In other words, you should not allow your feelings about one question to affect your success on the others. When you find a question that you either don't understand or don't know how to answer, just take a deep breath and do your best. Read the entire question slowly and carefully. Try rephrasing the question a couple of different ways. Then, read all of the answer choices carefully. After eliminating obviously wrong answers, make a selection and move on to the next question.

6. Confusing Answer Choices

When working on a difficult multiple-choice question, there may be a tendency to focus on the answer choices that are the easiest to understand. Many people, whether consciously or not, gravitate to the answer choices that require the least concentration, knowledge, and memory. This is a mistake. When you come across an answer choice that is confusing, you should give it extra attention. A question might be confusing because you do not know the subject matter to which it refers. If this is the case, don't eliminate the answer before you have affirmatively settled on another. When you come across an answer choice of this type, set it aside as you look at the remaining choices. If you can confidently assert that one of the other choices is correct, you can leave the confusing answer aside. Otherwise, you will need to take a moment to try to better understand the confusing answer choice. Rephrasing is one way to tease out the sense of a confusing answer choice.

7. Your First Instinct

Many people struggle with multiple-choice tests because they overthink the questions. If you have studied sufficiently for the test, you should be prepared to trust your first instinct once you have carefully and completely read the question and all of the answer choices. There is a great deal of research suggesting that the mind can come to the correct conclusion very quickly once it has obtained all of the relevant information. At times, it may seem to you as if your intuition is working faster even than your reasoning mind. This may in fact be true. The knowledge you obtain while studying may be retrieved from your subconscious before you have a chance to work out the associations that support it. Verify your instinct by working out the reasons that it should be trusted.

8. Key Words

Many test takers struggle with multiple-choice questions because they have poor reading comprehension skills. Quickly reading and understanding a multiple-choice question requires a mixture of skill and experience. To help with this, try jotting down a few key words and phrases on a piece of scrap paper. Doing this concentrates the process of reading and forces the mind to weigh the relative importance of the question's parts. In selecting words and phrases to write down, the test taker thinks about the question more deeply and carefully. This is especially true for multiple-choice questions that are preceded by a long prompt.

9. Subtle Negatives

One of the oldest tricks in the multiple-choice test writer's book is to subtly reverse the meaning of a question with a word like *not* or *except*. If you are not paying attention to each word in the question, you can easily be led astray by this trick. For instance, a common question format is, "Which of the following is...?" Obviously, if the question instead is, "Which of the following is not...?," then the answer will be quite different. Even worse, the test makers are aware of the potential for this mistake and will include one answer choice that would be correct if the question were not negated or reversed. A test taker who misses the reversal will find what he or she believes to be a correct answer and will be so confident that he or she will fail to reread the question and discover the original error. The only way to avoid this is to practice a wide variety of multiple-choice questions and to pay close attention to each and every word.

10. Reading Every Answer Choice

It may seem obvious, but you should always read every one of the answer choices! Too many test takers fall into the habit of scanning the question and assuming that they understand the question because they recognize a few key words. From there, they pick the first answer choice that answers the question they believe they have read. Test takers who read all of the answer choices might discover that one of the latter answer choices is actually *more* correct. Moreover, reading all of the answer choices can remind you of facts related to the question that can help you arrive at the correct answer. Sometimes, a misstatement or incorrect detail in one of the latter answer choices will trigger your memory of the subject and will enable you to find the right answer. Failing to read all of the answer choices is like not reading all of the items on a restaurant menu: you might miss out on the perfect choice.

11. Spot the Hedges

One of the keys to success on multiple-choice tests is paying close attention to every word. This is never more true than with words like *almost*, *most*, *some*, and *sometimes*. These words are called "hedges" because they indicate that a statement is not totally true or not true in every place and time. An absolute statement will contain no hedges, but in many subjects, like literature and history, the answers are not always straightforward or absolute. There are always exceptions to the rules in these subjects. For this reason, you should favor those multiple-choice questions that contain hedging language. The presence of qualifying words indicates that the author is taking special care with his or her words, which is certainly important when composing the right answer. After all, there are many ways to be wrong, but there is only one way to be right! For this reason, it is wise to avoid answers that are absolute when taking a multiple-choice test. An absolute answer is one that says things are either all one way or all another. They often include words like *every*, *always*, *best*, and *never*. If you are taking a multiple-choice test in a subject that doesn't lend itself to absolute answers, be on your guard if you see any of these words.

12. Long Answers

In many subject areas, the answers are not simple. As already mentioned, the right answer often requires hedges. Another common feature of the answers to a complex or subjective question are qualifying clauses, which are groups of words that subtly modify the meaning of the sentence. If the question or answer choice describes a rule to which there are exceptions or the subject matter is complicated, ambiguous, or confusing, the correct answer will require many words in order to be expressed clearly and accurately. In essence, you should not be deterred by answer choices that seem excessively long. Oftentimes, the author of the text will not be able to write the correct answer without offering some qualifications and modifications. Your job is to read the answer choices thoroughly and completely and to select the one that most accurately and precisely answers the question.

13. Restating to Understand

Sometimes, a question on a multiple-choice test is difficult not because of what it asks but because of how it is written. If this is the case, restate the question or answer choice in different words. This process serves a couple of important purposes. First, it forces you to concentrate on the core of the question. In order to rephrase the question accurately, you have to understand it well. Rephrasing the question will concentrate your mind on the key words and ideas. Second, it will present the information to your mind in a fresh way. This process may trigger your memory and render some useful scrap of information picked up while studying.

14. True Statements

Sometimes an answer choice will be true in itself, but it does not answer the question. This is one of the main reasons why it is essential to read the question carefully and completely before proceeding to the answer choices. Too often, test takers skip ahead to the answer choices and look for true statements. Having found one of these, they are content to select it without reference to the question above. Obviously, this provides an easy way for test makers to play tricks. The savvy test taker will always read the entire question before turning to the answer choices. Then, having settled on a correct answer choice, he or she will refer to the original question and ensure that the selected answer is relevant. The mistake of choosing a correct-but-irrelevant answer choice is especially common on questions related to specific pieces of objective knowledge, like historical or scientific facts. A prepared test taker will have a wealth of factual knowledge at his or her disposal, and should not be careless in its application.

15. No Patterns

One of the more dangerous ideas that circulates about multiple-choice tests is that the correct answers tend to fall into patterns. These erroneous ideas range from a belief that B and C are the most common right answers, to the idea that an unprepared test-taker should answer "A-B-A-C-A-D-A-B-A." It cannot be emphasized enough that pattern-seeking of this type is exactly the WRONG way to approach a multiple-choice test. To begin with, it is highly unlikely that the test maker will plot the correct answers according to some predetermined pattern. The questions are scrambled and delivered in a random order. Furthermore, even if the test maker was following a pattern in the assignation of correct answers, there is no reason why the test taker would know which pattern he or she was using. Any attempt to discern a pattern in the answer choices is a waste of time and a distraction from the real work of taking the test. A test taker would be much better served by extra preparation before the test than by reliance on a pattern in the answers.

FREE DVD OFFER

Don't forget that doing well on your exam includes both understanding the test content and understanding how to use what you know to do well on the test. We offer a completely FREE Test Taking Tips DVD that covers world class test taking tips that you can use to be even more successful when you are taking your test.

All that we ask is that you email us your feedback about your study guide. To get your **FREE Test Taking Tips DVD**, email freedvd@studyguideteam.com with "FREE DVD" in the subject line and the following information in the body of the email:

- The title of your study guide.
- Your product rating on a scale of 1-5, with 5 being the highest rating.
- Your feedback about the study guide. What did you think of it?
- Your full name and shipping address to send your free DVD.

Introduction to the SSAT Elementary Test

Function of the Test

The Secondary School Admission Test (SSAT) is a standardized test used for students applying to an independent or private school to determine if students have the necessary skills for success in a college preparatory program. The elementary level SSAT assesses basic math, verbal, reading, and writing skills in 3rd and 4th grade students who are applying to 4th and 5th grade. The test is administered nationwide in the US and is available in several other countries. The standard SSAT is administered on specific dates throughout the year. While middle and upper level SSATs allow for a Flex test administered on different dates, the Flex test is not available at the elementary level.

Test Administration

The standard SSAT is offered on 8 Saturdays throughout the year, with the elementary-level tests beginning in December. Sunday testing is available for religious reasons, but must be approved before registration. The test is available at hundreds of testing centers in the US and locations throughout the world. Students may only take the Flex SSAT once in an academic year, but can repeat the standard SSAT on any of the designated dates throughout the year. Elementary level students many only take the test twice in an academic year.

Students must create an account on the SSAT website in order to register. This account also allows students to print their admission tickets and receive their test scores. Registration opens about 10 weeks before a testing date, moving to late registration at 3 weeks before the test date and rush registration at 10 days before the test date. Additional fees are incurred for late and rush registration. Testing accommodations are available for students with disabilities. Students requiring accommodations must apply and be approved before registering for the test. Approval is only required once in an academic year.

Test Format

The elementary level SSAT is a four-part test consisting of multiple-choice questions in Quantitative (Math), Verbal, and Reading sections, and a writing sample. The writing sample is not scored. The Quantitative section includes 30 questions in the areas of addition, subtraction, multiplication, division, fractions, place value, and basic geometry and measurement. The Verbal section includes 30 questions in two categories: synonyms and analogies. The Reading section is divided into 7 passages, each with 4 questions, for a total of 28 questions. Questions focus mainly on reading comprehension, retention of information in the passage, and word meaning. The writing sample asks the student to write a respond to a picture with a story that has a beginning, middle, and end.

Section	Questions	Question Type	Time Allotted
Quantitative	30	Multiple Choice	30 minutes
Verbal	30	Multiple Choice	20 minutes
Break			15 minutes
Reading	28	Multiple Choice	30 minutes
Writing Sample	1	Written Response	15 minutes

Scoring

In the elementary level SSAT, there is no penalty for guessing. A free scoring report is available online through a student's SSAT account roughly 2 weeks after the test date. The report will include a narrative explanation of the scores, along with the number correct, percentage correct, a scaled score, percentile rank, and total scaled score. The possible scaled score ranges from 300 – 600. The percentile rank is from 1 – 99, and the total score is from 900 – 1800, with a mean of 1350. The SSAT is a norm-referenced test, meaning that the score is compared to a norm group of test takers' scores from the last 3 years. The score report will include the student's scores, as well as the average norm scores in each section for comparison. The percentile rank shows how a student did in comparison to the norm group. For example, if a student's percentile is 85, it means she scored the same or better than 85% of those in the norm group.

Recent/Future Developments

The SSAT testing accommodations were updated in the 2016-2017 academic year. The official guidelines for accommodations can be accessed on the SSAT.org website.

Quantitative Section

Basic Addition, Subtraction, Multiplication, and Division

Gaining more of something related to addition, while taking something away relates to subtraction. Vocabulary words such as *total, more, less, left,* and *remain* are common when working with these problems. The $+$ sign means plus. This shows that addition is happening. The $-$ sign means minus. This shows that subtraction is happening. The symbols will be important when you write out equations.

Addition can also be defined in equation form. For example, $4 + 5 = 9$ shows that $4 + 5$ is the same as 9. Therefore, $9 = 9$, and "four plus five equals nine." When two quantities are being added together, the result is called the *sum*. Therefore, the sum of 4 and 5 is 9. The numbers being added, such as 4 and 5, are known as the *addends*.

Subtraction can also be in equation form. For example, $9 - 5 = 4$ shows that $9 - 5$ is the same as 4 and that "9 minus 5 is 4." The result of subtraction is known as a *difference*. The difference of $9 - 5$ is 4. 4 represents the amount that is left once the subtraction is done. The order in which subtraction is completed does matter. For example, $9 - 5$ and $5 - 9$ do not result in the same answer. $5 - 9$ results in a negative number. So, subtraction does not adhere to the commutative or associative property. The order in which subtraction is completed is important.

Multiplication is when we add equal amounts. The answer to a multiplication problem is called a *product*. Products stand for the total number of items within different groups. The symbol for multiplication is $\times$ or $\cdot$. We say 2×3 or $2 \cdot 3$ means "2 times 3."

As an example, there are three sets of four apples. The goal is to know how many apples there are in total. Three sets of four apples gives $4 + 4 + 4 = 12$. Also, three times four apples gives $3 \times 4 = 12$. Therefore, for any whole numbers a and b, where a is not equal to zero, $a \times b = b + b + \cdots b$, where b is added a times. Also, $a \times b$ can be thought of as the number of units in a rectangular block consisting of a rows and b columns. For example, 3×7 is equal to the number of squares in the following rectangle:

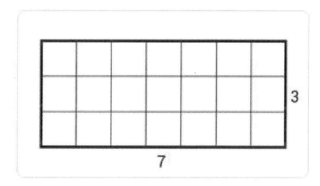

The answer is **21**, and there are 21 squares in the rectangle.

With any number times one (for example, $8 \times 1 = 8$) the original amount does not change. Therefore, one is the *multiplicative identity*. For any whole number a, $1 \times a = a$. Also, any number multiplied times zero results in zero. Therefore, for any whole number a, $0 \times a = 0$.

Division is based on dividing a given number into parts. The simplest problem involves dividing a number into equal parts. For example, a pack of 20 pencils is to be divided among 10 children. You would have to divide 20 by 10. In this example, each child would receive 2 pencils.

The symbol for division is $\div$ or $/$. The equation above is written as $20 \div 10 = 2$, or $20 / 10 = 2$. This means "20 divided by 10 is equal to 2." Division can be explained as the following: for any whole numbers a and b, where b is not equal to zero, $a \div b = c$ if and only if $a = b \times c$. This means, division can be thought of as a multiplication problem with a missing part. For instance, calculating $20 \div 10$ is the same as asking the following: "If there are 20 items in total with 10 in each group, how many are in each group?" Therefore, 20 is equal to ten times what value? This question is the same as asking, "If there are 20 items in total with 2 in each group, how many groups are there?" The answer to each question is 2.

In a division problem, a is known as the *dividend*, b is the *divisor*, and c is the *quotient*. Zero cannot be divided into parts. Therefore, for any nonzero whole number $a, 0 \div a = 0$. Also, division by zero is undefined. Dividing an amount into zero parts is not possible.

Harder division involves dividing a number into equal parts, but having some left over. An example is dividing a pack of 20 pencils among 8 friends so that each friend receives the same number of pencils. In this setting, each friend receives 2 pencils. There are 4 pencils leftover. 20 is the dividend, 8 is the divisor, 2 is the quotient, and 4 is known as the *remainder*. Within this type of division problem, for whole numbers a, b, c, and d, $a \div b = c$ with a remainder of d. This is true if and only if:

$$a = (b \times c) + d$$

When calculating $a \div b$, if there is no remainder, a is said to be *divisible* by b. *Even numbers* are all divisible by the number 2. *Odd numbers* are not divisible by 2. An odd number of items cannot be paired up into groups of 2 without having one item leftover.

Addition and subtraction are "inverse operations." Adding a number and then subtracting the same number will cancel each other out. This results in the original number, and vice versa. For example, $8 + 7 - 7 = 8$ and $137 - 100 + 100 = 137$.

Multiplication and division are also inverse operations. So, multiplying by a number and then dividing by the same number results in the original number. For example, $8 \times 2 \div 2 = 8$ and $12 \div 4 \times 4 = 12$. Inverse operations are used to work backwards to solve problems. In the case that 7 and a number add to 18, the inverse operation of subtraction is used to find the unknown value ($18 - 7 = 11$). If a school's entire 4th grade was divided evenly into 3 classes each with 22 students, the inverse operation of multiplication is used to determine the total students in the grade ($22 \times 3 = 66$). More scenarios involving inverse operations are listed in the tables below.

Word problems take concepts you learned in the classroom and turn them into real-life situations. Some parts of the problem are known and at least one part is unknown. There are three types of instances in which something can be unknown: the starting point, the change, or the final result. These can all be missing from the information they give you.

For an addition problem, the change is the quantity of a new amount added to the starting point.

For a subtraction problem, the change is the quantity taken away from the starting point.

Regarding addition, the given equation is $3 + 7 = 10$.

The number 3 is the starting point. 7 is the change, and 10 is the result from adding a new amount to the starting point. Different word problems can arise from this same equation, depending on which value is the unknown. For example, here are three problems:

- If a boy had 3 pencils and was given 7 more, how many would he have in total?
- If a boy had 3 pencils and a girl gave him more so that he had 10 in total, how many were given to him?
- A boy was given 7 pencils so that he had 10 in total. How many did he start with?

All three problems involve the same equation. Finding out which part of the equation is missing is the key to solving each word problem. The missing answers would be 10, 7, and 3.

In terms of subtraction, the same three scenarios can occur. The given equation is $6 - 4 = 2$.

The number 6 is the starting point. 4 is the change, and 2 is the new amount that is the result from taking away an amount from the starting point. Again, different types of word problems can arise from this equation. For example, here are three possible problems:

- If a girl had 6 quarters and 2 were taken away, how many would be left over?
- If a girl had 6 quarters, purchased a pencil, and had 2 quarters left over, how many did she pay with?
- If a girl paid for a pencil with 4 quarters and had 2 quarters left over, how many did she have to start with?

The three question types follow the structure of the addition word problems. Finding out whether the starting point, the change, or the final result is missing is the goal in solving the problem. The missing answers would be 2, 4, and 6.

The three addition problems and the three subtraction word problems can be solved by using a picture, a number line, or an algebraic equation. If an equation is used, a question mark can be used to show the number we don't know. For example, $6 - 4 = ?$ can be written to show that the missing value is the result. Using equation form shows us what part of the addition or subtraction problem is missing.

Key words within a multiplication problem involve *times, product, doubled,* and *tripled.* Key words within a division problem involve *split, quotient, divided, shared, groups,* and *half.* Like addition and subtraction, multiplication and division problems also have three different types of missing values.

Multiplication
Multiplication consists of a certain number of groups, with the same amount of items within each group, and the total amount within all groups. Therefore, each one of these amounts can be the missing value.

For example, the given equation is $5 \times 3 = 15$.

5 and 3 are interchangeable, so either amount can be the number of groups or the number of items within each group. 15 is the total number of items. Again, different types of word problems can arise from this equation.

For example, here are three problems:

- If a classroom is serving 5 different types of apples for lunch and has 3 apples of each type, how many total apples are there to give to the students?

- If a classroom has 15 apples with 5 different types, how many of each type are there?
- If a classroom has 15 apples with 3 of each type, how many types are there to choose from?

Each question involves using the same equation to solve. It is important to decide which part of the equation is the missing value. The answers to the problems are 15, 3, and 5.

Division

Similar to multiplication, division problems involve a total amount, a number of groups having the same amount, and a number of items within each group. The difference between multiplication and division is that the starting point is the total amount. It then gets divided into equal amounts.

For example, the equation is $15 \div 5 = 3$.

15 is the total number of items, which is being divided into 5 different groups. In order to do so, 3 items go into each group. Also, 5 and 3 are interchangeable. So, the 15 items could be divided into 3 groups of 5 items each. Therefore, different types of word problems can arise from this equation. For example, here are three types of problems:

- A boy needs 48 pieces of chalk. If there are 8 pieces in each box, how many boxes should he buy?
- A boy has 48 pieces of chalk. If each box has 6 pieces in it, how many boxes did he buy?
- A boy has partitioned all of his chalk into 8 piles, with 6 pieces in each pile. How many pieces does he have in total?

Each one of these questions involves the same equation. The third question can easily utilize the multiplication equation $8 \times 6 = ?$ instead of division. The answers are 6, 8, and 48.

Another method of multiplication can be done with the use of an *area model*. An area model is a rectangle that is divided into rows and columns that match up to the number of place values within each number. For example: $29 \times 65 = 25 + 4$ and $66 = 60 + 5$. The products of those 4 numbers are found within the rectangle and then summed up to get the answer. The entire process is:

$$(60 \times 25) + (5 \times 25) + (60 \times 4) + (5 \times 4) = 1{,}500 + 240 + 125 + 20 = 1{,}885$$

Here is the actual area model:

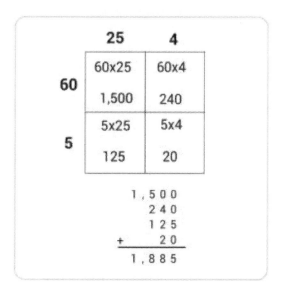

Decimals and fractions are two ways to represent positive numbers less than one. Counting money in coins is a good way to visualize values less than one. This is because problems dealing with change are stories that are used in real life. For example, if a student had 3 quarters and a dime and wanted to purchase a cookie at lunch for 50 cents, how much change would she receive? The answer would be found by first calculating the sum of the change as 85 cents and then subtracting 50 cents to get 35 cents. Money can also be used as a way to understand the transition between decimals and fractions. For example, a dime represents $0.10 or $\frac{1}{10}$ of a dollar. Problems involving both dollars and cents should also be considered. For example, if someone has 3 dollar bills and 2 quarters, the amount can be represented as a decimal as $3.50.

Formally, a *decimal* is a number that has a dot in the number. For example, 3.45 is a decimal. The dot is called a *decimal point*. The number to the left of the decimal point is in the ones place. The number to the right of the decimal point represents the part of the number less than one. The first number to the right of the decimal point is the tenths place, and one tenth represents $\frac{1}{10}$, just like a dime. The next place is the hundredths place, and it represents $\frac{1}{100}$, just like a penny. This idea is continued to the right in the hundredths, thousandths, and ten thousandths places. Each place value to the right is ten times smaller than the one to its left.

A number less than one has only digits in some decimal places. For example, 0.53 is less than one. A *mixed number* is a number greater than one that also contains digits in some decimal places. For example, 3.43 is a mixed number. Adding a zero to the right of a decimal does not change the value of the number. For example, 2.75 is the same as 2.750. However, 2.75 is the more accepted representation of the number. Also, zeros are usually placed in the ones column in any value less than one. For example, 0.65 is the same as .65, but 0.65 is more widely used.

In order to read or write a decimal, the decimal point is ignored. The number is read as a whole number. Then the place value unit is stated where the last digit falls. For example, 0.089 is read as *eighty-nine thousandths*, and 0.1345 is read as *one thousand, three hundred forty-five ten thousandths*. In mixed numbers, the word *and* is used to represent the decimal point. For example, 2.56 is read as *two and fifty-six hundredths*.

We multiply decimals the same way we multiply whole numbers. The only difference is that decimal places are included in the end result. For example, given the problem 87.5×0.45, the answer would be found by multiplying 875×45 to get 39,375. Then you would input a decimal point three places to the left because there are three total decimal places in the original problem. Therefore, the answer is 39.375.

Dividing a number by a single digit or two digits can be turned into repeated subtraction problems. An area model can be used throughout the problem that represents multiples of the divisor. For example, the answer to $8580 \div 55$ can be found by subtracting 55 from 8580 one at a time and counting the total number of subtractions necessary.

However, a simpler process involves using larger multiples of 55. First, $100 \times 55 = 5,500$ is subtracted from 8,580, and 3,080 is leftover. Next, $50 \times 55 = 2,750$ is subtracted from 3,080 to obtain 380. $5 \times 55 = 275$ is subtracted from 330 to obtain 55, and finally, $1 \times 55 = 55$ is subtracted from 55 to obtain zero. Therefore, there is no remainder, and the answer is $100 + 50 + 5 + 1 = 156$.

Here is a picture of the area model and the repeated subtraction process:

If you want to check the answer of a division problem, multiply the answer times the divisor. This will help you check to see if the dividend is obtained. If there is a remainder, the same process is done, but the remainder is added on at the end to try to match the dividend. In the previous example, $156 \times 64 = 9984$ would be the checking procedure. Dividing decimals involves the same repeated subtraction process. The only difference would be that the subtractions would involve numbers that include values in the decimal places. Lining up decimal places is crucial in this type of problem.

Order of Operations

When you're trying to solve a problem with more than one type of operation, there are certain steps to follow. These are called the order of operations. The different operations are parentheses, exponents, multiplication, division, addition, and subtraction. A common practice for remembering the order is the abbreviation "PEMDAS." This can be turned into "Please Excuse My Dear Aunt Sally". It should also be noted that multiplication and division are in the same rank and should be performed from left to right as they appear in the equation. The same goes for addition and subtraction. For example, solve the problem $8 - 2 \times 3 + 12 \div 4$. There are no parentheses or exponents in the problem. Therefore, we can go straight to the multiplication and division. After we multiply and divide, we are left with $8 - 6 + 3$. The addition and subtraction should be performed from left to right. This results in 5 as the answer.

Place Value

Numbers count in groups of 10. That number is the same throughout the set of natural numbers and whole numbers. It is referred to as working within a base 10 numeration system. Only the numbers from zero to 9 are used to represent any number. The foundation for doing this involves *place value*. Numbers are written side by side. This is to show the amount in each place value.

For place value, let's look at how the number 10 is different from zero to 9. It has two digits instead of just one. The one is in the tens' place, and the zero is in the ones' place. Therefore, there is one group of tens and zero ones. 11 has one 10 and one 1. The introduction of numbers from 11 to 19 should be the next step. Each value within this range of numbers consists of one group of 10 and a specific number of leftover ones. Counting by tens can be practiced once the tens column is understood. This process consists of increasing the number in the tens place by one. For example, counting by 10 starting at 17 would result in the next four values being 27, 37, 47, and 57.

A place value chart can be used for understanding and learning about numbers that have more digits. Here is an example of a place value chart:

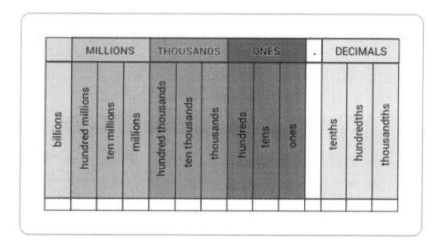

In the number 1,234, there are 4 ones and 3 tens. The 2 is in the hundreds' place, and the one is in the thousands' place. Note that each group of three digits is separated by a comma. The 2 has a value that is 10 times greater than the 3. Every place to the left has a value 10 times greater than the place to its right. Also, each group of three digits is also known as a *period*. 234 is in the ones' period.

The number 1,234 can be written out as *one-thousand, two hundred thirty-four*. The process of writing out numbers is known as the *decimal system*. It is also based on groups of 10. The place value chart is a helpful tool in using this system. In order to write out a number, it always starts with the digit(s) in the highest period. For example, in the number 23,815,467, the 23 is in highest place and is in the millions' period. The number is read *twenty-three million, eight hundred fifteen thousand, four hundred sixty-seven*. Each period is written separately through the use of commas. Also, no "ands" are used within the number. Another way to think about the number 23,815,467 is through the use of an addition problem. For example:

$$23,815,467 = 20,000,000 + 3,000,000 + 800,000 + 10,000 + 5,000 + 400 + 60 + 7$$

This expression is known as *expanded form*. The actual number 23,815,467 is known as being in *standard form*.

Rounding is an important concept dealing with place value. *Rounding* is the process of either bumping a number up or down, based on a certain place value. First, the place value is specified. Then, the digit to its right is looked at. For example, if rounding to the nearest hundreds place, the digit in the tens place is used. If it is a zero, one, 2, 3, or 4, the digit being rounded to is left alone. If it is a 5, 6, 7, 8 or 9, the digit being rounded to is increased by one. All other digits before the decimal point are then changed to zeros, and the digits in decimal places are dropped. If a decimal place is being rounded to, all digits that come after are just dropped. For example, if 845,231.45 was to be rounded to the nearest thousands place, the answer would be 845,000. The 5 would remain the same due to the 2 in the hundreds place. Also, if 4.567 were to be rounded to the nearest tenths place, the answer would be 4.6. The 5 increased to 6 due to the 6 in the hundredths place, and the rest of the decimal is dropped.

In order to compare whole numbers with many digits, place value can be used. In each number to be compared, it is necessary to find the highest place value in which the numbers differ and to compare the value within that place value. For example, $4,523,345 < 4,532,456$ because of the values in the ten thousands place. A similar process can be used for decimals. However, number lines can also be used. Tick marks can be placed within two whole numbers on the number line that represent tenths, hundredths, etc. Each number being compared can then be plotted. The leftmost value on the number line is the largest.

Mental math should always be considered as problems are worked through. It can save time to work a problem out in your head. If a problem is simple enough, such as $15 + 3 = 18$, it should be completed in your head. It will get easier to do this once you know addition and subtraction in higher place values. Mental math is also important in multiplication and division. The times tables, for multiplying all numbers from one to 12, should be memorized. This will allow for division within those numbers to be memorized as well. For example, $121 \div 11 = 11$ because it should be memorized that $11 \times 11 = 121$.

Here is the multiplication table to be memorized:

x	1	2	3	4	5	6	7	8	9	10	11	12	13	14	15
1	1	2	3	4	5	6	7	8	9	10	11	12	13	14	15
2	2	4	6	8	10	12	14	16	18	20	22	24	26	28	30
3	3	6	9	12	15	18	21	24	27	30	33	36	39	42	45
4	4	8	12	16	20	24	28	32	36	40	44	48	52	56	60
5	5	10	15	20	25	30	35	40	45	50	55	60	65	70	75
6	6	12	18	24	30	36	42	48	54	60	66	72	78	84	90
7	7	14	21	28	35	42	49	56	63	70	77	84	91	98	105
8	8	16	24	32	40	48	56	64	72	80	88	96	104	112	120
9	9	18	27	36	45	54	63	72	81	90	99	108	117	126	135
10	10	20	30	40	50	60	70	80	90	100	110	120	130	140	150
11	11	22	33	44	55	66	77	88	99	110	121	132	143	154	165
12	12	24	36	48	60	72	84	96	108	120	132	144	156	168	180
13	13	26	39	52	65	78	91	104	117	130	143	156	169	182	195
14	14	28	42	56	70	84	98	112	126	140	154	168	182	196	210
15	15	30	45	60	75	90	105	120	135	150	165	180	195	210	225

The values along the diagonal of the table consist of *perfect squares*. A perfect square is a number that represents a product of two equal integers.

A *number line* is a visual representation of all real numbers. It is a straight line on which any number can be plotted. The origin is zero, and the values to the right of the origin represent positive numbers. Values to the left of the origin represent negative numbers. Both sides extend forever. Here is an example of a number line:

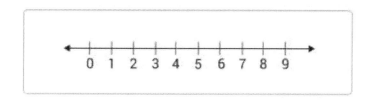

Number lines can be utilized for addition and subtraction. For example, it could be used to add $1 + 3$. Starting at one on the line, adding 3 to one means moving three units to the right to end up at 4. Therefore, $3 + 1$ is equal to 4. $5 - 2$ can also be determined. Start at 5 on the number line. Subtract 2 from 5. This means moving to the left two units from 5 to end up at 3. Therefore, $5 - 2$ is equal to 3.

The number line can also be used to show the identity property of addition and subtraction. What happens on the number line when you add or subtract zero? There is no movement along the line. For example, $5 + 0$ is equal to 5 and $4 - 0$ is equal to 4. Zero is known as both the *additive* and *subtractive identity*. This is because when you add or subtract zero from a number, that number does not change.

Addition adheres to the commutative property. This is because the order of the numbers being added does not matter. For example, both $4 + 5$ and $5 + 4$ equal 9. The *commutative property of addition* states that for any whole numbers a and b, it is true that $a + b = b + a$. Also, addition follows the associative property because the sum of three or more numbers results in the same answer, no matter what order the numbers are in. Let's look at the following example. Remember that numbers inside parentheses are always calculated first: $1 + (2 + 3)$ and $(1 + 2) + 3$ both equal 6. *The associative property of addition* states that for any whole numbers a, b, and c, $(a + b) + c = a + (b + c)$.

Ordering of Numbers

In counting, when a number appears after another number in order, that number will be one more. On the other hand, when a number appears before another number in order, that number will be one less. This idea is useful when counting backward. Also, zero means that there is none of something. This idea can be seen by taking away all of something so that there are zero items left. Also, learning to count by tens starting at any number is a key concept. Once a new number is learned, learning how to read and write that number is also important.

Placing numbers in an order in which they are listed from smallest to largest is known as *ordering*. When items are listed by using numbers in order, the *ordinal numbers*, 1st, 2nd, 3rd, 4th, ..., can be used.

When you order numbers the right way, you can more easily compare the different amounts of items. When you compare numbers you show whether two amounts are the same or different. Teachers can show two different quantities of items in the classroom. Then they can discuss which amount is lesser or greater. This exercise also can be used in order to classify numbers from the smallest amount to the largest amount.

Being able to compare any two whole numbers without a visual representation is also an important task. Each whole number relates to a certain amount. This amount can be ranked and compared to other amounts. Knowing the right vocabulary relating to ordering and comparing is important. The *equals sign* is $=$. It shows that two numbers are the same on either side of the symbol. For example, $28 = 28$. The symbols that are used for comparison are $<$ to represent *less than*, $>$ to represent *greater than*. The symbols $\leq$ to represent *less than or equal to*, and $\geq$ to represent *greater than or equal to*, and $\neq$ to represent *not equal to* can also be used.

You can compare numbers with any number of digits when you use these symbols. For example, the expression $77 < 100$, should be understood as 77 is less than 100. The expression $44 > 23$ should be understood as 44 is greater than 23. The expression $22 \neq 24$ should be understood as 22 is not equal *to* 24. Also, both $36 = 36$ and $36 \leq 36$ can be written because both "36 equals 36" and "36 is less than or equal to 36" applies.

Patterns

Patterns are an important part of mathematics. When mathematical calculations are completed repeatedly, patterns can be recognized. Recognizing patterns is an integral part of mathematics because it helps you understand relationships between different ideas. For example, a sequence of numbers can be given, and being able to recognize the relationship between the given numbers can help in completing the sequence.

For instance, given the sequence of numbers $7, 14, 21, 28, 35, \ldots$, the next number in the sequence would be 42. This is because the sequence lists all multiples of 7, starting at 7. Sequences can also be built from addition, subtraction, and division. Being able to recognize the relationship between the values that are given is the key to finding out the next number in the sequence.

Patterns within a sequence can come in 2 distinct forms. The items either repeat in a constant order, or the items change from one step to another in some consistent way. The core is the smallest unit, or number of items, that repeats in a repeating pattern. For example, the pattern ○○▲○○▲○... has a core that is ○○▲. Knowing only the core, the pattern can be extended. Knowing the number of steps in the core allows the identification of an item in each step without drawing/writing the entire pattern out. For example, suppose you must find the tenth item in the previous pattern. Because the core consists of three items (○○▲), the core repeats in multiples of 3. In other words, steps 3, 6, 9, 12, etc. will be ▲ completing the core with the core starting over on the next step. For the above example, the 9th step will be ▲ and the 10th will be ○.

The most common patterns where each item changes from one step to the next are arithmetic and geometric sequences. In an arithmetic sequence, the items increase or decrease by a constant difference. In other words, the same thing is added or subtracted to each item or step to produce the next. To determine if a sequence is arithmetic, see what must be added or subtracted to step one to produce step two. Then, check if the same thing is added/subtracted to step two to produce step three. The same thing must be added/subtracted to step three to produce step four, and so on. Consider the pattern 13, 10, 7, 4, ... To get from step one (13) to step two (10) by adding or subtracting requires subtracting by 3. The next step is checking if subtracting 3 from step two (10) will produce step three (7), and subtracting 3 from step three (7) will produce step four (4). In this case, the pattern holds true. Therefore, this is an arithmetic sequence in which each step is produced by subtracting 3 from the previous step. To extend the sequence, 3 is subtracted from the last step to produce the next. The next three numbers in the sequence are 1, -2, -5.

A geometric sequence is one in which each step is produced by multiplying or dividing the previous step by the same number. To see if a sequence is geometric, decide what step one must be multiplied or divided by to produce step two. Then check if multiplying or dividing step two by the same number produces step three, and so on. Consider the pattern 2, 8, 32, 128, ... To get from step one (2) to step two (8) requires multiplication by 4. The next step determines if multiplying step two (8) by 4 produces step three (32), and multiplying step three (32) by 4 produces step four (128). In this case, the pattern holds true. Therefore, this is a geometric sequence in which each step is found by multiplying the previous step by 4. To extend the sequence, the last step is multiplied by 4 and repeated. The next three numbers in the sequence are 512; 2,048; 8,192.

Arithmetic and geometric sequences can also be represented by shapes. For example, an arithmetic sequence could consist of shapes with three sides, four sides, and five sides. A geometric sequence could consist of eight blocks, four blocks, and two blocks (each step is produced by dividing the number of blocks in the previous step by 2).

<u>Relationships Between the Corresponding Terms of Two Numerical Patterns</u>
When given two number patterns, the corresponding terms should be examined to determine if a relationship exists between them. Corresponding terms between patterns are the pairs of numbers which appear in the same step of the two sequences. Consider the following patterns 1, 2, 3, 4,... and 3, 6, 9, 12, ... The corresponding terms are: 1 and 3; 2 and 6; 3 and 9; and 4 and 12. To identify the relationship, each pair of corresponding terms is examined. You can also examine the possibilities of performing an operation (+, −, ×, ÷) to each sequence. In this case:

$1 + 2 = 3$ or $1 \times 3 = 3$

$2 + 4 = 6$ or $2 \times 3 = 6$

$$3 + 6 = 9 \text{ or } 3 \times 3 = 9$$

$$4 + 8 = 12 \text{ or } 4 \times 3 = 12$$

The pattern is that the number from the first sequence multiplied by 3 equals the number in the second sequence. By assigning each sequence a label (input and output) or variable (x and y), the relationship can be written as an equation. The first sequence represents the inputs, or x, and the second sequence represents the outputs, or y. So, the relationship can be expressed as: $y = 3x$.

Consider the following sets of numbers:

a	2	4	6	8
b	6	8	10	12

To write a rule for the relationship between the values for a and the values for b, the corresponding terms (2 and 6; 4 and 8; 6 and 10; 8 and 12) are examined. The possibilities for producing b from a are:

$$2 + 4 = 6 \text{ or } 2 \times 3 = 6$$

$$4 + 4 = 8 \text{ or } 4 \times 2 = 8$$

$$6 + 4 = 10$$

$$8 + 4 = 12 \text{ or } 8 \times 1.5 = 12$$

The pattern is that adding 4 to the value of a produces the value of b. The relationship can be written as the equation $a + 4 = b$.

Basic Concepts of Geometry

Geometry is part of mathematics. It deals with shapes and their properties. Geometry means knowing the names and properties of shapes. It is also similar to measurement and number operations. The basis of geometry involves being able to label and describe shapes and their properties. That knowledge will lead to working with formulas such as area, perimeter, and volume. This knowledge will help to solve word problems involving shapes.

Flat or two-dimensional shapes include circles, triangles, hexagons, and rectangles, among others. Three-dimensional solid shapes, such as spheres and cubes, are also used in geometry. A shape can be classified based on whether it is open like the letter U or closed like the letter O. Further classifications involve counting the number of sides and vertices (corners) on the shapes. This will help you tell the difference between shapes.

Polygons can be drawn by sketching a fixed number of line segments that meet to create a closed shape. In addition, *triangles* can be drawn by sketching a closed space using only three line segments. *Quadrilaterals* are closed shapes with four line segments. Note that a triangle has three vertices, and a quadrilateral has four vertices.

To draw circles, one curved line segment must be drawn that has only one endpoint. This creates a closed shape. Given such direction, every point on the line would be the same distance away from its center. The radius of a circle goes from an endpoint on the center of the circle to an endpoint on the circle. The diameter is the line segment created by placing an endpoint on the circle, drawing through the radius, and placing the other endpoint on the circle. A compass can be used to draw circles of a more precise size and shape.

Area and Perimeter

Area relates to two-dimensional geometric shapes. Basically, a figure is divided into two-dimensional units. The number of units needed to cover the figure is counted. Area is measured using square units, such as square inches, feet, centimeters, or kilometers.

Perimeter is the length of all its sides. The perimeter of a given closed sided figure would be found by first measuring the length of each side and then calculating the sum of all sides.

Formulas can be used to calculate area and perimeter. The area of a rectangle is found by multiplying its length, *l,* times its width, *w.* Therefore, the formula for area is $A = l \times w$. An equivalent expression is found by using the term base, *b,* instead of length, to represent the horizontal side of the shape. In this case, the formula is $A = b \times h$. This same formula can be used for all parallelograms. Here is a visualization of a rectangle with its labeled sides:

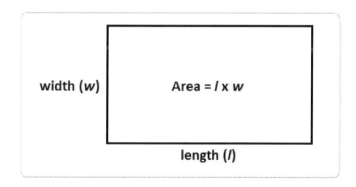

A square has four equal sides with the length *s.* Its length is equal to its width. The formula for the area of a square is $A = s \times s$. Finally, the area of a triangle is calculated by dividing the area of the rectangle that would be formed by the base, the altitude, and height of the triangle. Therefore, the area of a triangle is $A = \frac{1}{2} \times b \times h$. Formulas for perimeter are derived by adding length measurements of the sides of a figure. The perimeter of a rectangle is the result of adding the length of the four sides. Therefore, the formula for perimeter of a rectangle is $P = 2 \times l + 2 \times w$, and the formula for perimeter of a square is $P = 4 \times s$. The perimeter of a triangle would be the sum of the lengths of the three sides.

Volume

Volume is a measurement of the amount of space that in a 3-dimensional figure. Volume is measured using cubic units, such as cubic inches, feet, centimeters, or kilometers.

Say you have 10 playing die that are each one cubic centimeter. Say you placed these along the length of a rectangle. Then 8 die are placed along its width. The remaining area is filled in with die. There would be 80 die in total. This would equal a volume of 80 cubic centimeters. Say the shape is doubled so that its height consists of two cube lengths. There would be 160 cubes. Also, its volume would be 160 cubic centimeters. Adding another level of cubes would mean that there would be $3 \times 80 = 240$ cubes. This idea shows that volume is calculated by multiplying area times height. The actual formula for volume of a three-dimensional rectangular solid is $V = l \times w \times h$. In this formula *l* represents length, *w* represents width, and *h* represents height. Volume can also be thought of as area of the base times the height. The base in this case would be the entire rectangle formed by *l* and *w*. Here is an example of a rectangular solid with labeled sides:

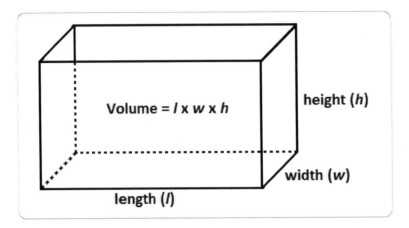

A *cube* is a special type of rectangular solid in which its length, width, and height are the same. If this length is *s*, then the formula for the volume of a cube is $V = s \times s \times s$.

Lines and Angles

In geometry, a *line* connects two points, has no thickness, and extends indefinitely in both directions beyond the points. If it does end at two points, it is known as a *line segment.* It is important to distinguish between a line and a line segment.

An angle can be visualized as a corner. It is defined as the formation of two rays connecting at a vertex that extend indefinitely. Angles are measured in degrees. Their measurement is a measure of rotation. A full rotation equals 360 degrees and represents a circle. Half of a rotation equals 180 degrees and represents a half-circle. Subsequently, 90 degrees represents a quarter-circle. Similar to the hands on a clock, an angle begins at the center point, and two lines extend indefinitely from that point in two different directions.

A clock can be useful when learning how to measure angles. At 3:00, the big hand is on the 12 and the small hand is on the 3. The angle formed is 90 degrees and is known as a *right angle.* Any angle less than 90 degrees, such as the one formed at 2:00, is known as an *acute angle.* Any angle greater than 90 degrees is known as an *obtuse angle.* The entire clock represents 360 degrees, and each clockwise increment on the clock represents an addition of 30 degrees. Therefore, 6:00 represents 180 degrees, 7:00 represents 210 degrees, etc. Angle measurement is additive. An angle can be broken into two non-overlapping angles. The total measure of the larger angle is equal to the sum of the measurements of the two smaller angles.

A *ray* is a straight path that has an endpoint on one end and extends indefinitely in the other direction. Lines are known as being *coplanar* if they are located in the same plane. Coplanar lines exist within the same two-dimensional surface. Two lines are *parallel* if they are coplanar, extend in the same direction, and never cross. They are known as being *equidistant* because they are always the same distance from each other. If lines do cross, they are known as *intersecting lines.* As discussed previously, angles are utilized throughout geometry, and their measurement can be seen through the use of an analog clock. An angle is formed when two rays begin at the same endpoint. *Adjacent angles* can be formed by forming two angles out of one shared ray. They are two side-by-side angles that also share an endpoint.

Perpendicular lines are coplanar lines that form a right angle at their point of intersection. A triangle that contains a right angle is known as a *right triangle*. The sum of the angles within any triangle is always 180 degrees. Therefore, in a right triangle, the sum of the two angles that are not right angles is 90 degrees. Any two angles that sum up to 90 degrees are known as *complementary angles*. A triangle that contains an obtuse angle is known as an *obtuse triangle*. A triangle that contains three acute angles is known as an *acute triangle*. Here is an example of a 180-degree angle, split up into an acute and obtuse angle:

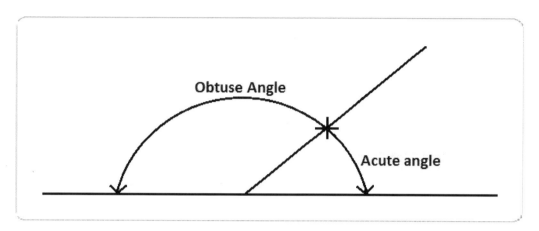

The vocabulary regarding many two-dimensional shapes is important to understand and use appropriately. Many four-sided figures can be identified using properties of angles and lines. A *quadrilateral* is a closed shape with four sides. A *parallelogram* is a specific type of quadrilateral that has two sets of parallel lines having the same length. A *trapezoid* is a quadrilateral having only one set of parallel sides. A *rectangle* is a parallelogram that has four right angles. A *rhombus* is a parallelogram with two acute angles, two obtuse angles, and four equal sides. The acute angles are of equal measure, and the obtuse angles are of equal measure. Finally, a *square* is a rhombus consisting of four right angles. It is important to note that some of these shapes share common attributes. For instance, all four-sided shapes are quadrilaterals. All squares are rectangles, but not all rectangles are squares.

Symmetry is another concept in geometry. If a two-dimensional shape can be folded along a straight line and the halves line up exactly, the figure is *symmetric*. The line is known as a *line of symmetry*. Circles, squares, and rectangles are examples of symmetric shapes.

Basic Concepts of Measurement

Measurement is how an object's length, width, height, weight, and so on, are quantified. Measurement is related to counting, but it is a more refined process.

The standard units of length in the United States are *inches*, *feet*, and *yards*. Weight units can vary, based on whether the substance being measured is a liquid or a solid. Standard units of weight to measure liquids include *ounces*, *pints*, *quarts*, and *gallons*. Occasionally, solids can also be measured using pints and quarts. For example, both milk and berries can be measured in pints. Other units of weight are *pounds* and *tons*.

The *metric* system is another measurement system. It is used in most countries outside of the United States. Units of mass within the metric system are *milligrams*, *grams*, and *kilograms*. Units of volume within the metric system are *milliliters* and *liters*. Finally, units of length within the metric system are *centimeters, meters,* and *kilometers.* Some other measures that are important are when you bake, such as *teaspoons, tablespoons,* and *cups,* or measuring temperature in *Celsius* and *Fahrenheit.* When discussing measurements, including proper units is crucial.

Telling time is another important measurement and real-world application. You should memorize units of time such as *seconds, minutes, hours, days,* and *years.* For example, there are 60 seconds in a minute, 60 minutes in each hour, and 24 hours in a day.

Converting units within either the United States units of measure or the metric system is important in real-world application problems. You should always make sure that values are converted to the same units before you begin the operation. If two lengths are added that have different units, the answer would not make sense. Some length conversions within the U.S. system are that one foot is 12 inches, one yard is 3 feet, and one mile is 5,280 feet. Some length conversions within the metric system are that one centimeter is 10 millimeters, one meter is 100 centimeters, and one kilometer is 1,000 meters. In terms of volume, one liter is 1,000 milliliters.

Tools, such as rulers, yardsticks, and measuring tapes, can be used to measure and compare the length of objects.

In order to determine the length of an object, it should be measured from end of the object to the other. Distance measurement is the same idea. Distance equals a measurement from the beginning to the end, with no gaps in between. Subtraction needs to be used to determine how much shorter an object is when compared to another object.

When you come across a measurement problem, pay attention to what units the final answer needs to be written in. All measurements should be converted to the same units before any calculations are completed. For example, if measurements are provided in both inches and feet, and the end result must be in inches, the measurements in feet must be converted to inches.

Interpretation of Graphs

Data can be represented in many ways including picture graphs, bar graphs, line plots, and tally charts. It is important to be able to organize the data into categories that could be represented using one of these methods. Equally important is the ability to read these types of diagrams and interpret their meaning.

A *picture graph* is a diagram that shows pictorial representation of data being discussed. The symbols used can represent a certain number of objects.

Notice how each fruit symbol in the following graph represents a count of two fruits. One drawback of picture graphs is that they can be less accurate if each symbol represents a large number. For example, if each banana symbol represented ten bananas, and students consumed 22 bananas, it may be challenging to draw and interpret two and one-fifth bananas as a frequency count of 22.

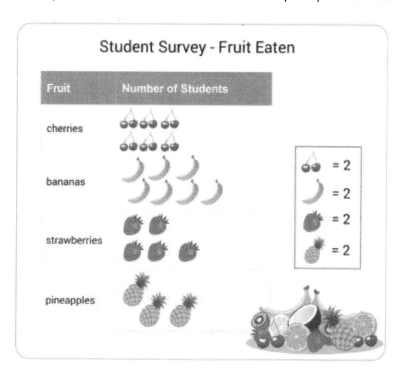

A *bar graph* is a diagram in which the quantity of items within a specific classification is represented by the height of a rectangle. Each type of classification is represented by a rectangle of equal width. Here is an example of a bar graph:

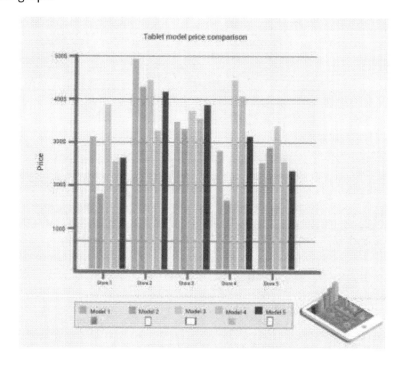

A *line plot* is a diagram that shows quantity of data along a number line. It is a quick way to record data in a structure similar to a bar graph without needing to do the required shading of a bar graph. Here is an example of a line plot:

A *tally chart* is a diagram in which tally marks are utilized to represent data. Tally marks are a means of showing a quantity of objects within a specific classification. Here is an example of a tally chart:

Number of days with rain	Number of weeks
0	||
1	𝍸
2	𝍸
3	𝍸
4	𝍸 𝍸 𝍸 ||||
5	𝍸 |
6	𝍸 |
7	||||

Data is often recorded using fractions, such as half a mile, and understanding fractions is critical because of their popular use in real-world applications. Also, it is extremely important to label values with their units when using data. For example, regarding length, the number 2 is meaningless unless it is attached to a unit. Writing 2 cm shows that the number refers to the length of an object.

A circle graph, also called a pie chart, shows categorical data with each category representing a percentage of the whole data set. To make a circle graph, the percent of the data set for each category must be determined. To do so, the frequency of the category is divided by the total number of data points and converted to a percent. For example, if 80 people were asked what their favorite sport is and

20 responded basketball, basketball makes up 25% of the data ($\frac{20}{80}=.25=25\%$). Each category in a data set is represented by a *slice* of the circle proportionate to its percentage of the whole.

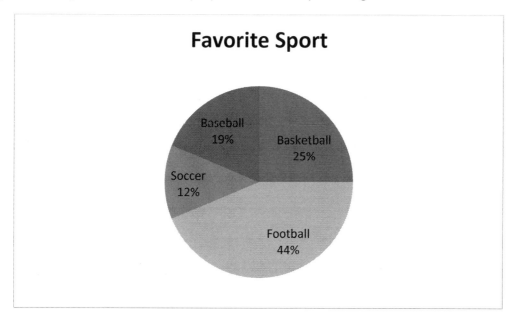

A scatter plot displays the relationship between two variables. Values for the independent variable, typically denoted by *x*, are paired with values for the dependent variable, typically denoted by *y*. Each set of corresponding values are written as an ordered pair (*x, y*). To construct the graph, a coordinate grid is labeled with the *x*-axis representing the independent variable and the *y*-axis representing the dependent variable. Each ordered pair is graphed.

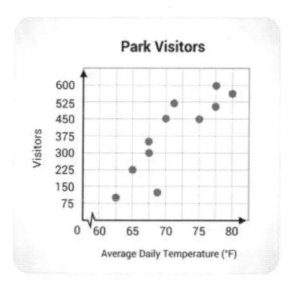

Like a scatter plot, a line graph compares two variables that change continuously, typically over time. Paired data values (ordered pair) are plotted on a coordinate grid with the *x*- and *y*-axis representing the two variables. A line is drawn from each point to the next, going from left to right. A double line graph simply displays two sets of data that contain values for the same two variables. The double line graph below displays the profit for given years (two variables) for Company A and Company B (two data sets).

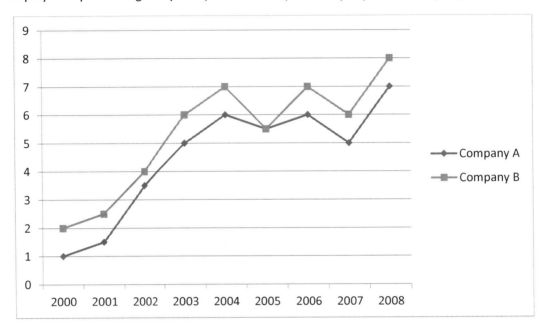

Choosing the appropriate graph to display a data set depends on what type of data is included in the set and what information must be shown. Histograms and box plots can be used for data sets consisting of individual values across a wide range. Examples include test scores and incomes. Histograms and box plots will indicate the center, spread, range, and outliers of a data set. A histogram will show the shape of the data set, while a box plot will divide the set into quartiles (25% increments), allowing for comparison between a given value and the entire set.

Scatter plots and line graphs can be used to display data consisting of two variables. Examples include height and weight, or distance and time. A correlation between the variables is determined by examining the points on the graph. Line graphs are used if each value for one variable pairs with a distinct value for the other variable. Line graphs show relationships between variables.

Practice Questions

1. Which of the following is equivalent to the value of the digit 3 in the number 792.134?

    a. 3×10

    b. 3×100

    c. $\dfrac{3}{10}$

    d. $\dfrac{3}{100}$

2. In the following expression, which operation should be completed first? $5 \times 6 + 4 \div 2 - 1$.

    a. Multiplication
    b. Addition
    c. Division
    d. Subtraction

3. How will the number 847.89632 be written if rounded to the nearest hundredth?

    a. 847.90
    b. 900
    c. 847.89
    d. 847.896

4. Which of the following is the definition of a prime number?

    a. A number that factors only into itself and one
    b. A number greater than zero that factors only into itself and one
    c. A number less than 10
    d. A number divisible by 10

5. Determine the next number in the following series: $1, 3, 6, 10, 15, 21, \ldots$

    a. 26
    b. 27
    c. 28
    d. 29

6. What of the following is the correct order of operations?

    a. Parentheses, Exponents, Multiplication, Division, Addition, Subtraction
    b. Exponents, Parentheses, Multiplication, Division, Addition, Subtraction
    c. Parentheses, Exponents, Addition, Multiplication, Division, Subtraction
    d. Parentheses, Exponents, Division, Addition, Subtraction, Multiplication

7. The perimeter of a 6-sided polygon is 56 cm. The length of three of the sides are 9 cm each. The length of two other sides are 8 cm each. What is the length of the missing side?

    a. 11 cm
    b. 12 cm
    c. 13 cm
    d. 10 cm

8. Which of the following is a mixed number?

    a. $16\frac{1}{2}$

    b. 16

    c. $\frac{16}{3}$

    d. $\frac{1}{4}$

9. If you were showing your friend how to round 245.2678 to the nearest thousandth, which place value would be used to decide whether to round up or round down?

    a. Ten-thousandth
    b. Thousandth
    c. Hundredth
    d. Thousand

10. Carey bought 184 pounds of fertilizer to use on her lawn. Each segment of her lawn required $12\frac{1}{2}$ pounds of fertilizer to do a sufficient job. If asked to determine how many segments could be fertilized with the amount purchased, what operation would be necessary to solve this problem?

    a. Multiplication
    b. Division
    c. Addition
    d. Subtraction

11. It is necessary to line up decimal places within the given numbers before performing which of the following operations?

    a. Multiplication
    b. Division
    c. Subtraction
    d. Fractions

12. Which of the following expressions best exemplifies the additive and subtractive identity?

    a. $5 + 2 - 0 = 5 + 2 + 0$
    b. $6 + x = 6 - 6$
    c. $9 - 9 = 0$
    d. $8 + 2 = 10$

13. What is an equivalent measurement for 1.3 cm?

    a. 0.13 m
    b. 0.013 m
    c. 0.13 mm
    d. 0.013 mm

14. Katie works at a clothing company and sold 192 shirts over the weekend. $\frac{1}{3}$ of the shirts that were sold were patterned, and the rest were solid. Which mathematical expression would calculate the number of solid shirts Katie sold over the weekend?

    a. $192 \times \frac{1}{3}$

    b. $192 \div \frac{1}{3}$

    c. $192 \times (1 - \frac{1}{3})$

    d. $192 \div 3$

15. Which four-sided shape is always a rectangle?

    a. Rhombus

    b. Square

    c. Parallelogram

    d. Quadrilateral

16. A rectangle was formed out of pipe cleaner. Its length was $\frac{1}{2}$ ft, and its width was $\frac{11}{2}$ inches. What is its area in square inches?

    a. $\frac{11}{4}$ inch^2

    b. $\frac{11}{2}$ inch^2

    c. 22 inch^2

    d. 33 inch^2

17. How will $\frac{4}{5}$ be written as a percent?

    a. 40 percent

    b. 125 percent

    c. 90 percent

    d. 80 percent

18. If Danny takes 48 minutes to walk 3 miles, how long should it take him to walk 5 miles maintaining the same speed?

    a. 32 min

    b. 64 min

    c. 80 min

    d. 96 min

19. Which of the following represents one hundred eighty-two million, thirty-six thousand, four hundred twenty-one and three hundred fifty-six thousandths?

    a. 182,036,421.356

    b. 182,036,421.0356

    c. 182,000,036,421.0356

    d. 182,000,036,421.356

20. A solution needs 5 ml of saline for every 8 ml of medicine given. How much saline is needed for 45 ml of medicine?

    a. $\frac{225}{8}$ ml

    b. 72 ml

    c. 28 m

    d. $\frac{45}{8}$ ml

21. What unit of volume is used to describe the following 3-dimensional shape?

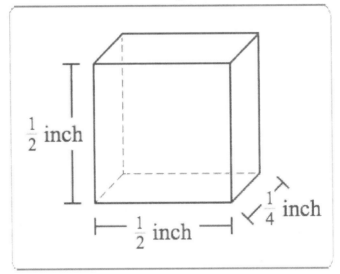

    a. Square inches
    b. Inches
    c. Cubic inches
    d. Squares

22. Which common denominator would be used in order to evaluate $\frac{2}{3} + \frac{4}{5}$?

    a. 15
    b. 3
    c. 5
    d. 10

23. In order to calculate the perimeter of a legal sized piece of paper that is 14 in and $8\frac{1}{2}$ in wide, what formula would be used?

    a. $P = 14 + 8\frac{1}{2}$

    b. $P = 14 + 8\frac{1}{2} + 14 + 8\frac{1}{2}$

    c. $P = 14 \times 8\frac{1}{2}$

    d. $P = 14 \times \frac{17}{2}$

24. Which of the following are units in the metric system?
    a. Inches, feet, miles, pounds
    b. Millimeters, centimeters, meters, pounds
    c. Kilograms, grams, kilometers, meters
    d. Teaspoons, tablespoons, ounces

25. Which important mathematical property is shown in the following expression?

$$(7 \times 3) \times 2 = 7 \times (3 \times 2)$$

    a. Distributive property
    b. Commutative property
    c. Associative property
    d. Multiplicative inverse

26. The diameter of a circle measures 5.75 centimeters. What tool could be used to draw such a circle?
    a. Ruler
    b. Meter stick
    c. Compass
    d. Yard stick

27. A piggy bank contains 12 dollars' worth of nickels. A nickel weighs 5 grams, and the empty piggy bank weighs 1050 grams. What is the total weight of the full piggy bank?
    a. 1,110 grams
    b. 1,200 grams
    c. 2,250 grams
    d. 2,200 grams

28. Last year, the New York City area received approximately $27\frac{3}{4}$ inches of snow. The Denver area received approximately 3 times as much snow as New York City. How much snow fell in Denver?
    a. 60 inches

    b. $27\frac{1}{4}$ inches

    c. $9\frac{1}{4}$ inches

    d. $83\frac{1}{4}$ inches

29. Which of the following would be an instance in which ordinal numbers are used?
    a. Katie scored a 9 out of 10 on her quiz.
    b. Matthew finished second in the spelling bee.
    c. Jacob missed one day of school last month.
    d. Kim was 5 minutes late to school this morning.

30. Evaluate $9 \times 9 \div 9 + 9 - 9 \div 9$.
    a. 0
    b. 17
    c. 81
    d. 9

Answer Explanations

1. D: $\frac{3}{100}$. Each digit to the left of the decimal point represents a higher multiple of 10 and each digit to the right of the decimal point represents a quotient of a higher multiple of 10 for the divisor. The first digit to the right of the decimal point is equal to the value ÷ 10. The second digit to the right of the decimal point is equal to the value ÷ (10 × 10), or the value ÷ 100.

2. A: Using the order of operations, multiplication and division are computed first from left to right. Multiplication is on the left; therefore, the teacher should perform multiplication first.

3. A: 847.90. The hundredth place value is located two digits to the right of the decimal point (the digit 9). The digit to the right of the place value is examined to decide whether to round up or keep the digit. In this case, the digit 6 is 5 or greater so the hundredth place is rounded up. When rounding up, if the digit to be increased is a 9, the digit to its left is increased by one and the digit in the desired place value is made a zero. Therefore, the number is rounded to 847.90.

4. B: A number is prime because its only factors are itself and one. Positive numbers (greater than zero) can be prime numbers.

5. C: Each number in the sequence is adding one more than the difference between the previous two. For example, $10 - 6 = 4, 4 + 1 = 5$. Therefore, the next number after 10 is $10 + 5 = 15$. Going forward, $21 - 15 = 6, 6 + 1 = 7$. The next number is $21 + 7 = 28$. Therefore, the difference between numbers is the set of whole numbers starting at 2: 2, 3, 4, 5, 6, 7, ...

6. A: Order of operations follows PEMDAS—Parentheses, Exponents, Multiplication and Division from left to right, and Addition and Subtraction from left to right.

7. C: Perimeter is found by calculating the sum of all sides of the polygon. $9 + 9 + 9 + 8 + 8 + s = 56$, where s is the missing side length. Therefore, 43 plus the missing side length is equal to 56. The missing side length is 13 cm.

8. A: $16\frac{1}{2}$. A mixed number contains both a whole number and either a fraction or a decimal. Therefore, the mixed number is $16\frac{1}{2}$.

9. A: The place value to the right of the thousandth place, which would be the ten-thousandth place, is what gets utilized. The value in the thousandth place is 7. The number in the place value to its right is greater than 4, so the 7 gets bumped up to 8. Everything to its right turns to a zero, to get 245.2680. The zero is dropped because it is part of the decimal.

10. B: This is a division problem because the original amount needs to be split up into equal amounts. The mixed number $12\frac{1}{2}$ should be converted to an improper fraction first.

$$12\frac{1}{2} = (12 \times 2) + \frac{1}{2} = \frac{23}{2}$$

Carey needs determine how many times $\frac{23}{2}$ goes into 184. This is a division problem:

$$184 \div \frac{23}{2} = ?$$

The fraction can be flipped, and the problem turns into the multiplication:

$$184 \times \frac{2}{23} = \frac{368}{23}$$

This improper fraction can be simplified into 16 because $368 \div 23 = 16$. The answer is 16 lawn segments.

11. C: Numbers should be lined up by decimal places before subtraction is performed. This is because subtraction is performed within each place value. The other operations, such as multiplication, division, and exponents (which is a form of multiplication), involve ignoring the decimal places at first and then including them at the end.

12. A: The additive and subtractive identity is zero. When added or subtracted to any number, zero does not change the original number.

13. B: 100 cm is equal to 1 m. 1.3 divided by 100 is 0.013. Therefore, 1.3 cm is equal to 0.013 mm. Because 1 cm is equal to 10 mm, 1.3 cm is equal to 13 mm.

14. C: $\frac{1}{3}$ of the shirts sold were patterned. Therefore, $1 - \frac{1}{3} = \frac{2}{3}$ of the shirts sold were solid. Anytime "of" a quantity appears in a word problem, multiplication needs to be used. Therefore:

$$192 \times \frac{2}{3} = 192 \times \frac{2}{3} = \frac{384}{3} = 128 \text{ solid shirts were sold}$$

The entire expression is $192 \times \left(1 - \frac{1}{3}\right)$.

15. B: A rectangle is a specific type of parallelogram. It has 4 right angles. A square is a rhombus that has 4 right angles. Therefore, a square is always a rectangle because it has two sets of parallel lines and 4 right angles.

16. D: Area = length x width. The answer must be in square inches, so all values must be converted to inches. $\frac{1}{2}$ ft is equal to 6 inches. Therefore, the area of the rectangle is equal to $6 \times \frac{11}{2} = \frac{66}{2} = 33$ square inches.

17. D: 80 percent. To convert a fraction to a percent, the fraction is first converted to a decimal. To do so, the numerator is divided by the denominator: $4 \div 5 = 0.8$. To convert a decimal to a percent, the number is multiplied by 100: $0.8 \times 10 = 80\%$.

18. C: 80 min. To solve the problem, a proportion is written consisting of ratios comparing distance and time. One way to set up the proportion is:

$$\frac{3}{48} = \frac{5}{x} \left(\frac{distance}{time} = \frac{distance}{time}\right)$$

x represents the unknown value of time. To solve a proportion, the ratios are cross-multiplied:

$$(3)(x) = (5)(48) \rightarrow 3x = 240$$

The equation is solved by isolating the variable, or dividing by 3 on both sides, to produce $x = 80$.

19. A: 182 is in the millions, 36 is in the thousands, 421 is in the hundreds, and 356 is the decimal.

20. A: Every 8 ml of medicine requires 5 ml. The 45 ml first needs to be split into portions of 8 ml. This results in $\frac{45}{8}$ portions. Each portion requires 5 ml. Therefore, $\frac{225}{8}$ ml are necessary.

$$\frac{45}{8} \times 5 = 45 \times \frac{5}{8} = \frac{225}{8} \text{ ml}$$

21. C: Volume of this 3-dimensional figure is calculated using length x width x height. Each measure of length is in inches. Therefore, the answer would be labeled in cubic inches.

22. A: A common denominator must be found. The least common denominator is 15 because it has both 5 and 3 as factors. The fractions must be rewritten using 15 as the denominator.

23. B: Perimeter of a rectangle is the sum of all four sides. Therefore, the answer is

$$P = 14 + 8\frac{1}{2} + 14 + 8\frac{1}{2} = 14 + 14 + 8 + \frac{1}{2} + 8 + \frac{1}{2} = 45 \text{ square inches}$$

24. C: Inches, pounds, and baking measurements, such as tablespoons, are not part of the metric system. Kilograms, grams, kilometers, and meters are part of the metric system.

25. C: It shows the associative property of multiplication. The order of multiplication does not matter, and the grouping symbols do not change the final result once the expression is evaluated.

26. C: A compass is a tool that can be used to draw a circle. The compass would be drawn by using the length of the radius, which is half of the diameter.

27. C: A dollar contains 20 nickels. Therefore, if there are 12 dollars' worth of nickels, there are $12 \times 20 = 240$ nickels. Each nickel weighs 5 grams. Therefore, the weight of the nickels is:

$$240 \times 5 = 1{,}200 \text{ grams}$$

Adding in the weight of the empty piggy bank, the filled bank weighs 2,250 grams.

28. D: 3 must be multiplied times $27\frac{3}{4}$. In order to easily do this, the mixed number should be converted into an improper fraction:

$$27\frac{3}{4} = 27 \times 4 + \frac{3}{4} = \frac{111}{4}$$

Therefore, Denver had approximately:

$$3 \times \frac{111}{4} = \frac{333}{4} \text{ inches of snow}$$

The improper fraction can be converted back into a mixed number through division:

$$\frac{333}{4} = 83\frac{1}{4} \text{ inches}$$

29. B: Ordinal numbers represent a ranking. Placing second in a competition is a ranking among the other participants of the spelling bee.

30. B: According to order of operations, multiplication and division must be completed first from left to right. Then, addition and subtraction is completed from left to right. Therefore:

$$9 \times 9 \div 9 + 9 - 9 \div 9$$

$$81 \div 9 + 9 - 9 \div 9$$

$$9 + 9 - 1$$

$$18 - 1$$

$$17$$

Verbal Section

Test takers encounter two parts in the verbal section of the Elementary SSAT. In the first part, the vocabulary section, questions address the test taker's understanding of language and the meanings of different words. The second part is the analogy section, which assesses the test taker's understanding of the finer details in the relationships of different words.

Vocabulary

Vocabulary is the words a person uses on a daily basis. Having a good vocabulary is important. It's important in writing and also when you talk to people. Many of the questions on the test may have words that you don't know. Therefore, it's important to learn ways to find out a word's meaning.

It's hard to use vocabulary correctly. Imagine being thrust into a foreign country. If you didn't know right words to use to ask for the things you need, you could run into trouble! Asking for help from people who don't share the same vocabulary is hard. Language helps us understand each other. The more vocabulary words a person knows, the easier they can ask for things they need. This section of the study guide focuses on getting to know vocabulary through basic grammar.

<u>Prefixes and Suffixes</u>
In this section, we will look at the *meaning* of various prefixes and suffixes when added to a root word. A *prefix* is a combination of letters found at the beginning of a word. A *suffix* is a combination of letters found at the end. A *root word* is the word that comes after the prefix, before the suffix, or between them both. Sometimes a root word can stand on its own without either a prefix or a suffix. More simply put:

Prefix + Root Word = Word

Root Word + Suffix = Word

Prefix + Root Word + Suffix = Word

Root Word = Word

Knowing the definitions of common prefixes and suffixes is helpful. It's helpful when you are trying to find out the meaning of a word you don't know. Also, knowing prefixes can help you find out the number of things, the negative of something, or the time and space of an object! Understanding suffixes can help when trying to find out the meaning of an adjective, noun, or verb.

The following charts look at some of the most common prefixes, what they mean, and how they're used to find out a word's meaning:

Number and Quantity Prefixes

Prefix	Definition	Example
bi-	two	bicycle, bilateral
mono-	one, single	monopoly, monotone
poly-	many	polygamy, polygon
semi-	half, partly	semiannual, semicircle
uni-	one	unicycle, universal

Here's an example of a number prefix:

The girl rode on a *bicycle* to school.

Look at the word *bicycle*. The root word (*cycle*)comes from the Greek and means *wheel*. The prefix *bi-* means *two*. The word *bicycle* means two wheels! When you look at any bicycles, they all have two wheels. If you had a unicycle, your bike would only have one wheel, because *uni-* means *one*.

Negative Prefixes

Prefix	Definition	Example
a-	without, lack of	amoral, atypical
in-	not, opposing	inability, inverted
non-	not	nonexistent, nonstop
un-	not, reverse	unable, unspoken

Here's an example of a negative prefix:

The girl was *insensitive* to the boy who broke his leg.

Look at the word *insensitive*. In the chart above, the prefix *in-* means *not* or *opposing*. Replace the prefix with *not*. Now place *not* in front of the word *sensitive*. Now we see that the girl was "not sensitive" to the boy who broke his leg. In simpler terms, she showed that she did not care. These are easy ways to use prefixes and suffixes in order to find out what a word means.

Time and Space Prefixes

Prefix	Definition	Example
a-	in, on, of, up, to	aloof, associate
ab-	from, away, off	abstract, absent
ad-	to, towards	adept, adjacent
ante-	before, previous	antebellum, antenna
anti-	against, opposing	anticipate, antisocial
cata-	down, away, thoroughly	catacomb, catalogue
circum-	around	circumstance, circumvent
com-	with, together, very	combine, compel
contra-	against, opposing	contraband, contrast
de-	from	decrease, descend
dia-	through, across, apart	diagram, dialect
dis-	away, off, down, not	disregard, disrespect
epi-	upon	epidemic, epiphany
ex-	out	example, exit
hypo-	under, beneath	hypoallergenic, hypothermia
inter-	among, between	intermediate, international
intra-	within	intrapersonal, intravenous
ob-	against, opposing	obtain, obscure
per-	through	permanent, persist
peri-	around	periodontal, periphery
post-	after, following	postdate, postoperative
pre-	before, previous	precede, premeditate
pro-	forward, in place of	program, propel
retro-	back, backward	retroactive, retrofit
sub-	under, beneath	submarine, substantial
super-	above, extra	superior, supersede
trans-	across, beyond, over	transform, transmit
ultra-	beyond, excessively	ultraclean, ultralight

Here's an example of a space prefix:

> The teacher's motivational speech helped *propel* her students toward greater academic achievement.

Look at the word *propel*. The prefix *pro-* means *forward*. *Forward* means something related to time and space. *Propel* means to drive or move in a forward direction. Therefore, knowing the prefix *pro-* helps interpret that the students are moving forward *toward greater academic achievement*.

Miscellaneous Prefixes

Prefix	Definition	Example
belli-	war, warlike	bellied, belligerent
bene-	well, good	benediction, beneficial
equi-	equal	equidistant, equinox
for-	away, off, from	forbidden, forsaken
fore-	previous	forecast, forebode
homo-	same, equal	homogeneous, homonym
hyper-	excessive, over	hyperextend, hyperactive
in-	in, into	insignificant, invasive
magn-	large	magnetic, magnificent
mal-	bad, poorly, not	maladapted, malnourished
mis-	bad, poorly, not	misplace, misguide
mor-	death	mortal, morgue
neo-	new	neoclassical, neonatal
omni-	all, everywhere	omnipotent, omnipresent
ortho-	right, straight	orthodontist, orthopedic
over-	above	overload, overstock,
pan-	all, entire	panacea, pander
para-	beside, beyond	paradigm, parameter
phil-	love, like	philanthropy, philosophic
prim-	first, early	primal, primer
re-	backward, again	reload, regress
sym-	with, together	symmetry, symbolize
vis-	to see	visual, visibility

Here's another prefix example:

The computer was *primitive*; it still had a floppy disk drive!

The word *primitive* has the prefix *prim-*. The prefix *prim-*indicates being *first* or *early*. *Primitive* means the early stages of evolution. It also could mean the historical development of something. Therefore, the sentence is saying that the computer is an older model, because it no longer has a floppy disk drive.

The charts that follow review some of the most common suffixes. They also include examples of how the suffixes are used to determine the meaning of a word. Remember, suffixes are added to the *end* of a root word:

Adjective Suffixes

Suffix	Definition	Example
-able (-ible)	capable of being	teachable, accessible
-esque	in the style of, like	humoresque, statuesque
-ful	filled with, marked by	helpful, deceitful
-ic	having, containing	manic, elastic
-ish	suggesting, like	malnourish, tarnish
-less	lacking, without	worthless, fearless
-ous	marked by, given to	generous, previous

Here's an example of an adjective suffix:

The live model looked so *statuesque* in the window display; she didn't even move!

Look at the word *statuesque*. The suffix *-esque* means *in the style of* or *like*. If something is *statuesque*, it's *like a statue*. In this sentence, the model looks like a statue.

Noun Suffixes

Suffix	Definition	Example
-acy	state, condition	literacy, legacy
-ance	act, condition, fact	distance, importance
-ard	one that does	leotard, billiard
-ation	action, state, result	legislation, condemnation
-dom	state, rank, condition	freedom, kingdom
-er (-or)	office, action	commuter, spectator
-ess	feminine	caress, princess
-hood	state, condition	childhood, livelihood
-ion	action, result, state	communion, position
-ism	act, manner, doctrine	capitalism, patriotism
-ist	worker, follower	stylist, activist
-ity (-ty)	state, quality, condition	community, dirty
-ment	result, action	empowerment, segment
-ness	quality, state	fitness, rudeness
-ship	position	censorship, leadership
-sion (-tion)	state, result	tension, transition
-th	act, state, quality	twentieth, wealth
-tude	quality, state, result	attitude, latitude

Look at the following example of a noun suffix:

The *spectator* cheered when his favorite soccer team scored a goal.

Look at the word *spectator*. The suffix *-or* means *action*. In this sentence, the *action* is to *spectate* (watch something). Therefore, a *spectator* is someone involved in watching something.

Verb Suffixes

Suffix	Definition	Example
-ate	having, showing	facilitate, integrate
-en	cause to be, become	frozen, written
-fy	make, cause to have	modify, rectify
-ize	cause to be, treat with	realize, sanitize

Here's an example of a verb suffix:

The preschool had to *sanitize* the toys every Tuesday and Thursday.

In the word *sanitize*, the suffix *-ize* means *cause to be* or *treat with*. By adding the suffix *-ize* to the root word *sanitary*, the meaning of the word becomes active: *cause to be sanitary*.

Context Clues

It's common to findwords that aren't familiar in writing. When you don't know a word, there are some "tricks" that can be used to find out its meaning. *Context clues* are words or phrases in a sentence or paragraph that provide hints about a word and what it means. For example, if an unknown word is attached to a noun with other surrounding words as clues, these can help you figure out the word's meaning. Consider the following example:

After the treatment, Grandma's natural rosy cheeks looked *wan* and ghostlike.

The word we don't know is *wan.* The first clue to its meaning is in the phrase *After the treatment,* which tells us that something happened after a procedure (possibly medical). A second clue is the word *rosy,* which describes Grandma's natural cheek color that changed after the treatment. Finally, the word *ghostlike* infers that Grandma's cheeks now look white. By using the context clues in the sentence, we can figure out that the meaning of the word *wan* means *pale.*

Below are more ways to use context clues to find out the meaning of a word we don't know:

Contrasts

Look for context clues that *contrast* the unknown word. When reading a sentence with a word we don't know, look for an opposite word or idea. Here's an example:

Since Mary didn't cite her research sources, she lost significant points for *plagiarizing* the content of her report.

In this sentence, *plagiarizing* is the word we don't know. Notice that when Mary *didn't cite her research sources,* it resulted in her losing points for *plagiarizing the content of her report.* These contrasting ideas tell us that Mary did something wrong with the content. This makes sense because the definition of *plagiarizing* is "taking the work of someone else and passing it off as your own."

Contrasts often use words like *but, however, although,* or phrases like *on the other hand.* For example:

The *gargantuan* television won't fit in my car, but it will cover the entire wall in the den.

The word we don't know is *gargantuan.* Notice that the television is too big to fit in a car, *but it will cover the entire wall in the den.* This tells us that the television is extremely large. The word *gargantuan* means *enormous.*

Synonyms

Another way to find out a word you don't know is to think of synonyms for that word. Synonyms are words with the same meaning. To do this, replace synonyms one at a time. Then read the sentence after each synonym to see if the meaning is clear. By replacing a word we don't know with a word we do know, it's easier to uncover its meaning. For example:

Gary's clothes were *saturated* after he fell into the swimming pool.

In this sentence, we don't know the word *saturated*. To brainstorm synonyms for *saturated*, think about what happens to Gary's clothes after falling into the swimming pool. They'd be *soaked* or *wet*. These both turn out to be good synonyms to try. The actual meaning of *saturated* is "thoroughly soaked."

Antonyms

Sometimes sentences contain words or phrases that oppose each other. Opposite words are known as *antonyms*. An example of an antonym is *hot* and *cold*. For example:

Although Mark seemed *tranquil,* you could tell he was actually nervous as he paced up and down the hall.

The word we don't know is *tranquil.* The sentence says that Mark was in fact not *tranquil.* He was *actually nervous.* The opposite of the word *nervous* is *calm. Calm* is the meaning of the word *tranquil.*

Explanations or Descriptions

Explanations or descriptions of other things in the sentence can also provide clues to an unfamiliar word. Take the following example:

Golden Retrievers, Great Danes, and Pugs are the top three *breeds* competing in the dog show.

We don't know the word *breeds*. Look at the sentence for a clue. The subjects (*Golden Retrievers, Great Danes,* and *Pugs*) describe different types of dogs. This description helps uncover the meaning of the word *breeds.* The word *breeds* means "a particular type of animal."

Inferences

Inferences are clues to an unknown word that tell us its meaning. These inferences can be found within the sentence where the word appears. Or, they can be found in a sentence before the word or after the word. Look at the following example:

The *wretched* old lady was kicked out of the restaurant. She was so mean and nasty to the waiter!

Here, we don't know the word *wretched*. The first sentence says that the *old lady was kicked out of the restaurant*, but it doesn't say why. The sentence after tells us why: *She was so mean and nasty to the waiter!* This infers that the old lady was *kicked out* because she was *so mean and nasty* or, in other words, *wretched*.

When you prepare for a vocabulary test, try reading harder materials to learn new words. If you don't know a word on the test, look for prefixes and suffixes to find out what the word means and get rid of wrong answers. If two answers both seem right, see if there are any differences between them. Then select the word that best fits. Context clues in the sentence or paragraph can also help you find the meaning of a word you don't know. By learning new words, a person can expand their knowledge. They can also improve the quality of their writing.

Analogies

Analogies compare two different things that are related to each other. For example, a basic analogy is: apple is to fruit as cucumber is to vegetable. This analogy points out the category each item belongs to. On the SSAT, the final term (vegetable, in this case) will be blank. The blank must be filled in from the choices. You must select the word that best shows the relationship in the first pair of words.

Other analogies include words that are synonyms. Synonyms are words that mean the same thing. For example, *big* and *large* are synonyms. *Tired* and *sleepy* are also synonyms. Verbal analogy questions can be hard. After practice, you will see small differences between word meanings and how they connect to each other.

Not all analogies are synonyms. Some analogies are *antonyms,* or words that are opposites. One example of an antonym is: fast as to slow as high is to low. Fast is the opposite of slow, and high is the opposite of low.

Analogies can also tell us the characteristics of things. An example of this is: pickle is to salty as candy is to sweet. Here the adjectives (salty and sweet) describe qualities of the foods.

Analogies also include people who use things and things that are used. For example: crayon is to draw as axe is the chop. This gives us a tool and then tells us what it is used for. The tools may also be linked tithe person who uses the device. For example, brush is to painter as hoe is to farmer. Painters use brushes to paint and farmers use hoes on the farm. Similarly, products are often linked to their producer. An example is: muffin is to baker as statue is to sculpture. The test taker must be familiar with the occupations to pick the right relationship.

Other analogies link parts of an object to the whole. An example is: fingers are to hand as toes are to foot. Or, bark is to tree as husk is to corn. With this last category mentioned, test takers must try to establish the precise relationship between the first two items when choosing the missing item in the second pair. For example, consider the following analogy and answer choices:

Bark is to tree as _____ is to hand.
  a. Fingers
  b. Skin
  c. Leaves
  d. Finger nails

Without thinking carefully, test takers may select Choice *A*: fingers. After all, trees *have* bark and hands *have* fingers. However, the relationship between bark and the tree should be more precisely defined as this: bark *covers* the tree. Then, careful test takers would select Choice *B*: skin. Skin covers the hand just like bark covers the tree.

The last types of analogy on the SSAT have to do with *homonyms* or rhyming words. Homonyms are words that are spelled differently but they sound the same. An example is four and for or bear and bare.

An analogy with rhyming words may *be sound is to pound as chair is to bear.* Sometimes it is helpful to read the analogies out loud quietly. The relationship may be in how the words sound, which can be harder to imagine.

It's also important to pay attention to the word order of each analogy question. Let's look at the following difficult question:

Carpenter is to saw as _____.

    a. Paint is to brush

    b. Painter is to mural

    c. Painter is to brush

    d. Brush is to painter

The correct answer is *C*: painter is to brush, because carpenters use saws for their tools and painters use brushes. Choice *D* reverses the order of the tool and the user, making the analogy false.

Practice Questions

Synonyms

Each of the questions below has one word. The one word is followed by five words or phrases. Please select one answer whose meaning is closest to the word in capital letters.

1. WEARY:
    a. tired
    b. clothing
    c. happy
    d. hot
    e. whiny

2. VAST:
    a. Rapid
    b. Expansive
    c. Small
    d. Ocean
    e. Uniform

3. DEMONSTRATE:
    a. Tell
    b. Show
    c. Build
    d. Complete
    e. Make

4. ORCHARD:
    a. Flower
    b. Fruit
    c. Grove
    d. Peach
    e. Farm

5. TEXTILE:
    a. Fabric
    b. Document
    c. Mural
    d. Ornament
    e. Knit

6. OFFSPRING:
    a. Bounce
    b. Parent
    c. Music
    d. Child
    e. Skip

7. PERMIT:
   a. Law
   b. Parking
   c. Crab
   d. Jail
   e. Allow

8. INSPIRE:
   a. Motivate
   b. Impale
   c. Exercise
   d. Patronize
   e. Collaborate

9. WOMAN:
   a. Man
   b. Lady
   c. Women
   d. Girl
   e. Mother

10. ROTATION:
   a. Wheel
   b. Year
   c. Spin
   d. Flip
   e. Orbit

11. CONSISTENT:
   a. Stubborn
   b. Contains
   c. Sticky
   d. Texture
   e. Steady

12. PRINCIPLE:
   a. Principal
   b. Leader
   c. President
   d. Foundation
   e. Royal

13. PERIMETER:
   a. Outline
   b. Area
   c. Side
   d. Volume
   e. Inside

14. SYMBOL:
    a. Drum
    b. Music
    c. Clang
    d. Emblem
    e. Text

15. GERMINATE:
    a. Doctor
    b. Sick
    c. Infect
    d. Plants
    e. Grow

Analogies

The questions below ask you to find relationships between words. For each question, select the answer that best completes the meaning of the sentence.

16. Wheel is to truck as:
    a. Foot is to body
    b. Steering wheel is to car
    c. Truck is to road
    d. Head is to body
    e. Boat is to river

17. Open is to closed as above is to:
    a. Shut
    b. On top
    c. Next to
    d. Beyond
    e. Below

18. Cow is to milk as:
    a. Horse is to cow
    b. Egg is to chicken
    c. Chicken is to egg
    d. Glass is to milk
    e. Milk is to glass

19. Web is to spider as den is to:
    a. Living room
    b. Eagle
    c. Fox
    d. Dog
    e. Turtle

20. Sad is to blue as happy is to:
    a. Glad
    b. Yellow
    c. Smiling
    d. Laugh
    e. Calm

21. Door is to store as deal is to:
    a. Money
    b. Purchase
    c. Sell
    d. Wheel
    d. Market

22. Dog is to veterinarian as baby is to
    a. Daycare
    b. Mother
    c. Puppy
    d. Babysitter
    e. Pediatrician

23. Clock is to time as:
    a. Ruler is to length
    b. Jet is to speed
    c. Alarm is to sleep
    d. Drum is to beat
    e. Watch is to wrist

24. Ice is to slippery as rug is to:
    a. Soft
    b. Carpet
    c. Floor
    d. Hard
    e. Mop

25. Calf is to cow as foal is to:
    a. Gerbil
    b. Monkey
    c. Horse
    d. Goat
    e. Sheep

26. Wire is to electricity as:
    a. Power is to lamp
    b. Pipe is to water
    c. Fire is to heat
    d. Heat is to fire
    e. Water is to pipe

27. Currency is to money as:
    a. Paper is to plastic
    b. Rich is to poor
    c. Dollars are to cents
    d. Length is to width
    e. Story is to tale

28. Cat is to paws as
    a. Giraffe is to neck
    b. Elephant is to ears
    c. Horse is to hooves
    d. Snake is to skin
    e. Chicken is to feathers

29. Falcon is to mice as giraffe is to
    a. Leaves
    b. Rocks
    c. Antelope
    d. Grasslands
    e. Neck

30. President is to Executive Branch as _____ is to Judicial Branch.
    a. Supreme Court Justice
    b. Judge
    c. Senator
    d. Lawyer
    e. Congressmen

Answer Explanations

1. A: Weary most closely means tired. Someone who is weary and tired may be whiny, but they do not necessarily mean the same thing.

2. B: Something that is vast is big and expansive. Choice *D*, ocean, may be described as vast. However, the word itself does not mean vast. The heavens or skies may also be described as vast. Someone's imagination or vocabulary can also be vast.

3. B: To demonstrate something means to show it. A demonstration is a show-and-tell type of example. It is usually visual.

4. C: An orchard is most like a grove. Both are areas like plantations that grow different kinds of fruit. Peach is a type of fruit that may be grown in an orchard. However, *peach* is not a synonym for orchard. Many citrus fruits are grown in groves. But either word can be used to describe many fruit-bearing trees in one area. Choice *E*, farm, may have an orchard or grove on the property. However, they are not the same thing, and many farms do not grow fruit trees.

5. A: A textile is another word for a fabric. The most confusing choice in this case is Choice *E*, knit. This is because some textiles are knit, but *textile* and *knit* are not synonym. Plenty of textiles are not knit.

6. D: Offspring are the kids of parents. This word is common when talking about the animal kingdom. Though it can be used with humans as well. *Offspring* does have the word *spring* in it. But it has nothing to do with bounce, Choice *A*. Choice *B*, parent, maybe tricky because parents have offspring. But for this reason, they are not synonyms.

7. E: Permit can be a verb or a noun. As a verb, it means to allow or give permission for something. As a noun, it refers to a document or something that has been authorized like a parking permit or driving permit. This would allow the authorized person to park or drive under the rules of the document.

8. A: If someone is inspired, they are driven to do something. Someone who is an inspiration motivates others to follow their lead.

9. B: A woman is a lady. You must read carefully and remember the difference between *woman* and *women*. *Woman* refers to one person who is female. *Women* is the plural form and refers to more than one, or a group, of ladies. A woman can be a mother, but not necessarily. *Woman* and *mother* are not synonyms. A girl is a child and not yet a woman.

10. C: Rotation means to spin or turn, like a wheel rotating on a car. But *wheel*, Choice *A*, does not mean the same thing as the word *rotation*.

11. E: Something that is consistent is steady, predictable, reliable, or constant. The tricky ones here is that the word *consistency* comes from the word consistent. *Consistency* may describe a texture or something that is sticky, Choices *C* and *D*. *Consistent* also comes from the word *consist*. *Consist* means to contain (Choice *B*). You must know some vocabulary to recognize the differences in these words.

12. D: A principle is a guiding idea or belief. Someone with good moral character is described as having strong principles. You must be careful not to get confused with the homonyms *principle* and *principal*, Choice *A*. These two words have different meanings. A principal is the leader of a school. The word principal also refers to the main idea or most important thing.

13. A: Perimeter refers to the outline of an object. You may recognize that word from math class. In math class, perimeter refers to the edges or distance around a closed shape. Some of the other choices refer to other math words encountered in geometry. However, they do not have the same meaning as *perimeter.*

14. D: A symbol is an object, picture, or sign that is used to represent something. For example, a pink ribbon is a symbol for breast-cancer awareness. A flag can be a symbol for a country. The tricky part of this question was also knowing the meaning of *emblem. Emblem* describes a design that represents a group or concept, much like a symbol. Emblems often appear on flags or a coat of arms.

15. E: Germinate means to develop or grow. It most often refers to sprouting seeds as a new plant first breaks through the seed coat. It can also refer to the development of an idea. Choice *D, plants,* may be an attractive choice since plants germinate. However, the word *germinate* does not mean *plant.*

16. A: The best fit here is wheel is to truck as foot is to body. Wheels are the part of the truck that make contact with the ground to roll the vehicle forward. Feet are the part of the body that walk on the ground during locomotion.

17. E: Open and closed are opposites, so the question is looking for the opposite of *above*. Choices *A* (shut), *C* (next to), and *D* (beyond) are not opposites. Choice *B* (on top) is a synonym of above, so it may be tricky but it is not correct. The opposite or antonym for above is *below*.

18. C: Cows produce milk so the question is looking for another pair that has a producer and their product. Horses don't produce cows (Choice *A*), glasses don't produce milk (Choice *D*) and milk doesn't produce a glass (Choice *E*). The correct choice is *C*: chicken is to egg. The tricky one here is Choice *B*, egg is to chicken, because it has the correct words but the wrong order; therefore, it reverses the relationship. Eggs don't produce chickens so it does not work with the first part of the analogy: cow is to milk.

19. C: The first part of the analogy – web is to spider – describes the home (web) and who lives in it (spider), so the question is looking for what animal lives in a den. The best choice is *C*, fox. Living room, Choice *A*, is a synonym for a den.

20. A: Sad and blue are synonyms because they both describe the same type of mood. The word *blue* in this case is not referring to the color. Therefore, although Choice *B*, yellow, is sometimes considered a "happy" color, the question isn't referring to blue as a color. Yellow and happy are not synonyms. Someone who is happy may laugh or smile, Choices *C* and *D*. However, these words are not synonyms for happy. Lastly, someone who is happy may be calm, Choice *E*, although they could also be excited. Calm and happy are not synonyms. The best choice is glad.

21. D: The key to answering this question correctly is to recognize the relationship between door and store. Door and store are both words that rhyme. You might be thinking that stores have doors. However, after seeing the other word choices and the given word *deal*, you should notice that none of the other words have this relationship. Instead, the answer should rhyme with *deal*. Wheel and deal, although spelled differently, are rhyming words. Therefore, the correct answer is *D*.

22. E: This question tests your knowledge of jobs. Dogs are taken care of by veterinarians. So the solution is looking for who takes care of babies. However, mothers and babysitters, Choices *B* and *D*, can also take care of babies. Veterinarians take care of sick dogs and act as a medical doctor for pets. Therefore, with this higher level of detail, test takers should select pediatrician. Pediatricians are doctors for babies and children.

23. A: The relationship in the first half of the analogy is that clocks are used to measure time. The second half of the analogy should have a tool that is used to measure something followed by what it measures. Rulers can be used to measure length. So Choice *A* is the best choice. Remember that the key to solving analogies is to be a good detective. Some of the other answer choices are related to clocks and time but not to the relationship *between* clocks and time.

24. A: *Slippery* is an adjective that describes the surface of ice. The answer is best filled by a word that describes rugs, such as soft (Choice *A*). Carpet, Choice *B*, is a synonym for a rug rather than an adjective that describes rugs. Therefore, that is an incorrect choice. Rugs cover the floor, Choice *C*, so again, this is not an adjective for a rug and not the correct answer. Hard, Choice *D*, is an adjective, but the opposite of describing a rug. Mop, Choice *E*, is not correct, as it does not describe rugs.

25. C: A calf is a baby cow and a foal is a baby horse. Choice *C* is the only answer choice that makes sense.

26. B: Wires are the medium that carry electricity, allowing the current to flow in a circuit. Pipes carry water in a similar fashion. So the best choice is *B*. You must be careful to not select Choice *E*, water is to pipe. This reverses the relationship between the two. Choices *A*, *C*, and *D* contain words that are related to one another but not in the same way as wires and electricity.

27. E: Currency and money have the same meaning. Currency is a word used to describe the money in a country or region. Therefore, the best choice is *E*. Astor and a tale mean the same thing.

28. C: This is a part/whole analogy. The common thread is what animals walk on. Choices *A*, *B*, and *E* all describe certain parts of animals. However, paws are not the defining feature of cats. While snakes travel on their skin, they do not walk.

29. A: This is a provider/provision analogy. The theme of this analogy is pairing a specific animal to their food source. Falcons prey on mice. Giraffes are herbivores and only eat one of the choices: leaves. Grasslands, Choice *D*, describe a type of landscape, not a food source for animals.

30. A: This question asks you to know the basic roles and positions of the three branches of the government. The president serves in the Executive Branch and the Supreme Court Justices serve in the Judicial Branch.

Reading Section

In the Reading section, you will have seven short passages. Each passage has four multiple-choice questions. The passages may be poetry, fiction, and nonfiction writing from many subjects. You may be asked to find word definitions or main ideas and supporting details. You may also be asked what literal language is opposed to non literal language.

Reading comprehension is being able to understand what you've read. Reading skills include fluency, vocabulary knowledge, and background knowledge. Fluency is the pace at which one reads. Background knowledge is the information you know about the passage before you've read it. These are all great building blocks that good readers use.

Good readers practice these skills before, during, and after reading. Before readers go through a passage, they should ask the following questions: "What do I already know about this subject?" and "What will the book be about?" While reading the passage, you should imagine the text. You should also use new information to make predictions. You can make connections to a personal experience. Or you can connect what you've read to another story. After reading a passage, you should be able to summarize the main idea. Good readers are able to retell the story in their own words.

Six Types of Comprehension Strategies

1. QUESTION	2. CONNECT	3. INFER
Monitor reading by asking questions before, during, and after reading a passage. "What if?," "I don't understand why," or "Maybe when" are all examples of how to use questions while reading.	Use knowledge to help with understanding text. Connecting with other stories or experiences is a way to help with reading comprehension. "This reminds me of … because" and "When I heard … it reminds me of" are both examples of how to connect with passages.	When authors do not give a clear answer, it sometimes helps to infer what happens in the passage. Inferring helps with making predictions, drawing conclusions, and reflecting on text. "I think," "Maybe," and "Perhaps" are all examples of ways to infer while reading.
4. VISUALIZE	**5. WHAT'S IMPORTANT**	**6. SYNTHESIZE**
Create pictures in the mind about the text. "I see," "It must have smelled like," and "I can imagine" are all examples of how to visualize while reading.	Determine the author's main idea. "The main idea is," "This section is mainly about," and "It is important to remember" are all examples of how to determine what is important while reading.	Combine current knowledge with new information to help with text understanding. "After reviewing," "At first I thought," and "Now I think" are all examples of how to synthesize information while reading.

Topic Versus the Main Idea

It is important to know the difference between the topic and the main idea of the passage. Even though these two are similar, they have some differences. A topic is the subject of the text. It can usually be described in a one- to two-word phrase. On the other hand, the main idea is more detailed. It provides the author's central point of the passage. It can be expressed through a complete sentence. It is often found in the beginning, middle, or end of a paragraph. In most nonfiction books, the first sentence of the passage usually states the main idea. Take a look at the passage below to review the topic versus the main idea.

> Cheetahs are one of the fastest mammals on land, reaching up to seventy miles an hour over short distances. Even though cheetahs can run as fast as seventy miles an hour, they usually only have to run half that speed to catch up with their choice of prey. Cheetahs cannot maintain a fast pace over long periods of time because they will overheat their bodies. After a chase, cheetahs need to rest for approximately thirty minutes prior to eating or returning to any other activity.

In the example above, the topic of the passage is Cheetahs because that is the subject of the text. The main idea of the text is "Cheetahs are one of the fastest mammals on the land but can only maintain a fast pace for shorter distances." While this covers the topic, it is more detailed. It refers to the text in its entirety. The passage provides more details called supporting details. These will be discussed in the next section.

Supporting Details

Supporting details help you understand the main idea. Supporting details answer questions like *who, what, where, when, why,* and *how.* Supporting details can include examples, facts, statistics, small stories, and visual details.

Persuasive and informative texts often use supporting details. In persuasive texts, authors try to make readers agree with their points of view. In persuasive texts, supporting details are often used as "selling points." If authors say something, they should support it with evidence. This helps to persuade readers. Informative texts use supporting details to inform readers. Take another look at the "Cheetahs" example from the page before to find examples of supporting details.

In the Cheetah example above, supporting details include:

- Cheetahs reach up to seventy miles per hour over short distances.
- Cheetahs usually only have to run half that speed to catch up with their prey.
- Cheetahs will overheat their bodies if they exert a high speed over longer distances.
- They need to rest for thirty minutes after a chase.

Look at the diagram below (applying the cheetah example) to help determine the hierarchy of topic, main idea, and supporting details.

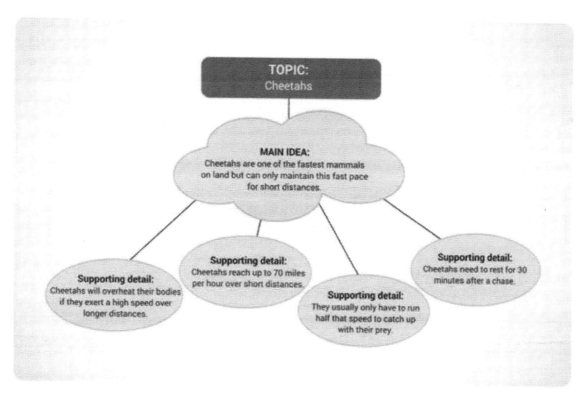

Theme

The theme is the central message of the story. The theme can be about a moral or lesson that the author wants to share with the readers. Although authors do not directly state the theme of a story, it is the "big picture" that they want readers to walk away with. For example, the fairy tale "The Boy Who Cried Wolf" is the tale of a little boy who always lied about seeing a wolf. When the little boy really saw a wolf, no one believed him. The author of this fairy tale does not tell readers, "Don't lie because people will question the truth of the story." However, the author presents this moral through the tale.

The themeof a text can center around varying subjects such as courage, friendship, love, bravery, facing challenges, or adversity. It often leaves readers with more questions than answers. Authors tend to imply certain themes in texts. However, readers are left to find out the true meaning of the story.

Purposes for Writing

Authors want readers to like their story. A good reader listens to what an author has to say. An author's purpose may be to persuade, inform, entertain, or be descriptive. Most stories are written to entertain the reader. Some stories may also be informative or persuasive. When an author wants to persuade the reader, the reader must be careful. The author may want to keep the persuasion lighthearted and friendly to maintain the entertainment. However, the author may still be trying to convince the reader of something, even if the story seems just for fun.

Informative texts means that the author is trying to educate the reader on a certain topic. Informative texts are usually nonfiction, which means they are true. The author doesn't state their opinion in an informative text. They simply tell you the facts to inform you. Some informative texts have headings, subtitles and bold key words. The purpose of informative texts is to educate the reader.

Entertaining texts can be fiction or nonfiction. They are meant to capture your attention. Entertaining texts are stories that describe real or fictional people, places or things. These stories use exciting language, emotion, and imagery. They also use figurative language. If an author writes a good entertaining text, you will never want to put the book down!

Descriptive texts describe people, places, or things to show a clear image to the reader. If an author fails to show these details, readers may find it boring or confusing. Descriptive texts are almost always informative. But they can also be persuasive or entertaining. It depends on the author's purpose.

Writing Devices

Authors use a variety of writing devices throughout texts. Below is a list of some writing devices authors use in their writing.

- Comparison and Contrast
- Cause and Effect
- Analogy
- Point of View
- Transitional Words and Phrases

Let's look at each device individually.

Comparison and Contrast

One writing device authors use is comparison and contrast. Comparison is when authors take objects and show how they are the same. Contrast is when authors take objects and show how they differ. Comparison and contrast essays are mostly written in nonfiction form. There are common words used when authors compare or contrast. The list below will show you some of these words:

Comparison Words:

- Similar to
- Alike
- As well as
- Both

Contrast Words:

- Although
- On the other hand
- Different from
- However
- As opposed to
- More than
- Less than
- On the contrary

Cause and Effect

Cause and effect is a common writing device. A cause is why something happens. An effect is something that happens because of the cause. Many times, authors use key words to show cause and effect, such as *because, so, therefore, without, now, then,* and *since*. For example:"Because of the sun shower, a rainbow appeared." In this sentence, due to the sun shower (the cause), a rainbow appeared (the effect).

Analogy

An analogyis a comparison between two things. Sometimes the two things are very different from one another. Authors often use analogiesto add meaning and make ideas relatable in texts. There are two types of analogies: metaphors and similes. Metaphors compare two things that are not similar. Similes also compare two unlike things but use the words *like* or *as*. For example, "In the library, students are asked to be as quiet as a mouse." Clearly, students and mice are very different. However, when students are asked to be as quiet as a mouse, readers understand that they are being asked to be absolutely silent.

Point of View

Point of view is the viewpoint in which authors tell stories. Authors can tell stories in either the first or third person. If an author writes in the first person, they are a character within a story telling about their own experiences. The pronouns *I* and *we* are used when writing in the first person. If an author writes in the third person, the narrator is telling the story from an outside perspective. The author is not a character in the story, but rather tells about the characters' actions and dialogues. Pronouns such as *he,she,it,* and *they* are used in texts written in the third person.

Transitional Words and Phrases
There are approximately 200 transitional words and phrases that are commonly used in the English language. Below are lists of common transition words and phrases.

Time	Example	Compare	Contrast	Addition	Logical Relationships	Steps
after	for example	likewise	however	and	if	first
before	in fact	also	yet	also	then	second
during	for instance		but	furthermore	therefore	last
in the middle				moreover	as a result	
					since	

Transitional words and phrases are important writing devices. They connect sentences and paragraphs. Transitional words and phrases help writing to make more sense. They provide clearer meaning to readers.

Fiction

Fiction is imaginative text that is invented by the author. Fiction is characterized by the following literary elements:

- Characters: the people, animals, aliens, or other living figures the story is about
- Setting: the location, surroundings, and time the story takes place in
- Conflict: a problem that the characters face either internally or externally
- Plot: the sequence and the rise and fall of excitement in the action of a story
- Resolution: the solution to the conflict that is discovered as a result of the story
- Point of View: the lens through which the reader experiences the story
- Theme: the moral to the story or the message the author is sending to the reader

Historical Fiction
Historical fiction is a story that occurs in the past. It uses real settings and characters. Historical fiction can have true events mixed in with events that are made up.

Science Fiction
Science fiction is an invented story. It occurs in the future or in a different world. It often deals with space, time travel, robots, or aliens. It sometimes has highly advanced technology.

Fantasy
Fantasy involves magic or supernatural elements. It can take place in an imaginary world. Examples include talking animals, superheroes rescuing the day, or characters taking on a mythical journey or quest.

Mystery and Adventure
Mystery fiction is a story that involves a puzzle or crime to be solved by the main characters. The mystery is driven by suspense. The reader must sort through clues and distractions to solve the puzzle with the main character. Adventure stories are driven by the risky or exciting action that happens in the plot.

Realistic and Contemporary Fiction

Realistic fiction is when the author shows the world within the story without question. The characters are ordinary. The action could happen in real life. The conflict often involves growing up, family life, or learning to cope with emotion.

Nonfiction Literature

Nonfiction writing is true in detail. Nonfiction can cover almost any topic in the natural world. Nonfiction writers do research and gather facts before writing. Nonfiction has the following subgenres (or subcategories):

Informational text: This is written to tell information to the reader. It may have charts, graphs, indexes, glossaries, or bibliographies.

Persuasive text: This is meant to sway the reader to have a certain opinion or to take action.

Biographies and Autobiographies: Biographies tell details of someone's life. If an author writes the text about someone else, it is a biography. If the author writes it about them self, it is an autobiography.

Communicative text: This is used for the purpose of communicating with another person. This includes emails, formal and informal letters, and tweets. This content often consists of two-sided chats between people.

Drama

Drama is any writing that is meant to be performed in front of an audience, such as plays, TV, and movie scripts.

Comedy: Comedy is any drama designed to be funny or lighthearted.

Tragedy: Tragedy is any drama designed to be serious or sad.

Poetry

Poetry is written in verse and often has rhythm. It often involves descriptive imagery, rhyming stanzas, and a beautiful mastery of language. It is often personal, emotional, and reflective. Poetry is often considered a work of art.

Folklore

Folklore is writing that has been handed down from generation to generation by word of mouth. Folklore is often not based in fact but in fanciful beliefs. Folklore is very important to a culture or custom.

Fairy Tales: These are usually written for children and often carry a moral or universal truth. They are stories written about fairies or other magical creatures.

Fables: Similar to fairy tales, fables are written for children and include tales of supernatural people or animals that speak like people.

Myths: Myths are often about the gods, include symbolism, and may involve historical events and reveal human behavior. Sometimes they tell how historical things came about.

Legends: Exaggerated and only partially truthful, these are tales of heroes and important events.

Tall Tales: Often funny stories and sometimes set in the Wild West, these are tales that contain extreme exaggeration.

Interpreting Words and Phrases

Words can have different meanings depending on how they are used in a text. Once a reader knows the correct meaning and how to say a word, they can better understand the context of the word. There are lots of methods for helping readers solve word meanings.

Dictionary: Dictionaries are not allowed on the test. However, readers should know how to use a dictionary and a thesaurus. In dictionaries, there can be more than one meaning for a certain word. Dictionaries also help teach how to say words. A thesaurus teaches words that have the same meanings (synonyms) and words that have opposite meanings (antonyms).

Word Parts: Separating words into their word parts, (root word, prefix, suffix) will help determine the meaning of a word as a whole.

Context Clues: Readers can look at other words in sentences to help them find out the meaning of an unknown word by the way it is used in the same sentence or paragraph. This kind of search provides context clues.

Author's Purpose: Authors use words differently depending on what they want the reader to learn. Some ways writers use words are as follows:

- Literal: the exact meaning of the word
- Figurative: metaphorical language and figures of speech
- Technical: in-depth writing about certain subjects like math or music
- Connotative: showing an opinion in the text as a secondary meaning

Determining Text Structures

Text structures are used for different reasons in writing. Each text structure has key words and elements that help identify it. Readers use text structure to help find information within a text. Summarizing requires knowledge of the text structure of a piece of writing. Here are some common text structures:

Chronological Order: Time order or sequence from one point to another. Dates and times might be used, or bullets and numbering. Possible key words: *first, next, then, after, later, finally, before, preceding, following*

Cause and Effect: Showing how causes lead to effects. Possible key words: *cause, effect, consequently, as a result, due to, in order to, because of, therefore, so, leads to, if/then*

Problem and Solution: Talks about a problem in detail and gives solutions to the problem. Possible key words: *difficulty, problem, solve, solution, possible, therefore, if/then, challenge*

Compare and Contrast: Talks about how objects, people, places, and ideas might be the same or different from each other. Possible key words: *like, unlike, similar to, in contrast, on the other hand, whereas, while, although, either or, opposed to, different from, instead*

Description: Explains a topic with the main idea and details. Possible key words: *for example, such as, for instance, most importantly, another, such as, next to, on top of, besides*

Inference

When readers put together clues from the writing to "guess" that a certain idea is a fact, it is called making inferences. Making inferences helps read "between the lines" of the writing. Readers read "between the lines" to figure out why the author wrote what they wrote.

Inferences are about being able to make wise guesses based on clues from the writing. People make inferences about the world around them every day. However, they may not be aware of what they are doing. For example, a young boy may infer that it is cold outside if he wakes up and his bedroom is chilly. Or, a girl is driving somewhere and she sees a person on the side of the road with a parked car. The girl might think that person's car broke down, and that they are waiting for help. Both of these are examples of how inferences are used every day.

Making inferences is kind of like being a detective. Sometimes clues can be found in the pictures that are inside of a story. For example, a story might show a picture of a school where all the children are in the parking lot. Looking more closely, readers might spot a fire truck parked at the side of the road and might infer that the school had a fire drill or an actual fire.

Summarizing

Readers can summarize writing to find out the main idea in a passage. This helps readers remember what they read and retell the main idea in their own words. Summarizing can sometimes be hard to do. Summarizing means figuring out what's most important in the passage and getting rid of the words that are not important. Summarizing also means taking the first passage and making it smaller. Summarizing uses many of the reader's skills.

Practice Questions

Read the following passage, and then answer questions 1-4.

Do you want to vacation at a Caribbean island destination? Who wouldn't want a tropical vacation? Visit one of the many Caribbean islands where visitors can swim in crystal blue waters, swim with dolphins, or enjoy family-friendly resorts and activities. Every island offers a unique and dazzling vacation destination. Choose from these islands: Aruba, St. Lucia, Barbados, Anguilla, St. John, and so many more. A Caribbean island destination will be the best and most refreshing vacation ever ... no regrets!

1. What is the topic of the passage?
    a. Caribbean island destinations
    b. Tropical vacation
    c. Resorts
    d. Activities

2. What is/are the supporting detail(s) of this passage?
    a. Cruising to the Caribbean
    b. Local events
    c. Family activities
    d. All of the above

Read the following sentence, and answer the question below.

"A Caribbean island destination will be the best and most refreshing vacation ever ... no regrets!"

3. What is this sentence an example of?
    a. Fact
    b. Opinion
    c. Device
    d. Fallacy

4. What is the author's purpose of this passage?
    a. Entertain readers
    b. Persuade readers
    c. Inform or teach readers
    d. Share a moral lesson to readers

Read the following passage, and then answer questions 5-8.

Even though the rain can put a damper on the day, it can be helpful and fun, too. For one, the rain helps plants grow. Without rain, grass, flowers, and trees would be deprived of vital nutrients they need to develop. Not only does the rain help plants grow, but on days where there are brief spurts of sunshine, rainbows can appear. The rain reflects and refracts the light, creating beautiful rainbows in the sky. Finally, puddle jumping is another fun activity that can be done in or after the rain. Therefore, the rain can be helpful and fun.

5. What is the *cause* in this passage?
   a. Plants growing
   b. Rainbows
   c. Puddle jumping
   d. Rain

Read the following sentence, and answer the question below.

"Without rain, grass, flowers, and trees would be deprived of vital nutrients they need to develop."

6. In this sentence, the author is using what literary device regarding the grass, flowers, and trees?
   a. Comparing
   b. Contrasting
   c. Describing
   d. Transitioning

7. In the same sentence from above, what is most likely the meaning of *vital?*
   a. Energetic
   b. Truthful
   c. Necessary
   d. Dangerous

8. What is an *effect* in this passage?
   a. Rain
   b. Brief spurts of sunshine
   c. Rainbows
   d. Weather

Read the following passage, and then answer questions 9-12.

Lola: The Siberian Husky

Meet Lola. Lola is an overly friendly Siberian husky who loves her long walks, digs holes for days, and sheds unbelievably . . . like a typical Siberian husky. Lola has to be brushed and brushed and brushed— did I mention that she has to be brushed all the time! On her long walks, Lola loves making friends with new dogs and kids. A robber could break into our house, and even though they may be intimidated by Lola's wolf-like appearance, the robber would be shocked to learn that Lola would most likely greet them with kisses and a tail wag. She makes friends with everyone! Out of all the dogs we've ever owned, Lola is certainly one of a kind in many ways.

9. Based on the passage, what does the author imply?
   a. Siberian huskies are great pets but require a lot of time and energy.
   b. Siberian huskies are easy to take care of.
   c. Siberian huskies should not be around children.
   d. Siberian huskies are good guard dogs.

10. What word best describes the author of this passage because of their own experience with Siberian huskies?
    a. Impartial
    b. Hasty
    c. Biased
    d. Irrational

11. Based on the passage, we can infer what about Lola's owner (the narrator)?
    a. It is a man.
    b. It is a woman.
    c. It is a new dog owner.
    d. It is an experienced dog owner.

12. Based on the information in the passage, which of the following dogs most likely looks like Lola?

a.

b.

c.

d.

Read the following passage, and then answer questions 13-16.

Learning how to write a ten-minute play may seem like a challenging task at first; but, if you follow a simple creative writing strategy, similar to writing a story, you will be able to write a successful drama. The first step is to open your story as if it is a puzzle to be solved. This will allow the reader to engage with the story and to solve the story with you, the author. Immediately provide descriptive details that set the main idea, the tone, and the mood according to the theme you have in mind. Next, use dialogue to reveal the attitudes and personalities of each of the characters who have a key part in the unfolding story. Show images on stage to speed up the dialogue; remember, one picture speaks a thousand words. As the play progresses, the protagonist must cross the point of no return in some way; this is the climax of the story. Then, as in a written story, you create a resolution to the life-changing event of the protagonist.

13. Based on the passage above, select the statement that is true.
    a. Writing a ten-minute play is very difficult.
    b. Providing descriptive details is not necessary.
    c. The climax of the story sets the theme you have in mind.
    d. Descriptive details give clues to the play's intended mood and tone.

14. Which of the following is the most likely meaning for the phrase "one picture speaks a thousand words" in the following sentence?

"Show images on stage to speed up the dialogue; remember, one picture speaks a thousand words."

    a. Audio-video technology should be used to enhance scenery in a play.
    b. Playwrights should be sure to add videos to speed up the dialogue.
    c. Pictures can tell stories as well, if not better, than words.
    d. Playwrights should include an image after every 1000 words of dialogue.

15. What is the meaning of the word *protagonist?*
    a. Main character
    b. Actor
    c. Student
    d. Playwright

16. In the passage above, the writer suggests that writing a ten-minute play is doable for a new playwright for which of the following reasons?

    a. It took the author of the passage only one week to write their first play.
    b. The format follows similar strategies of writing a narrative story.
    c. There are no particular themes or points to unravel in a ten-minute play.
    d. Dialogue is not necessary if you have images.

Read the following passage, and then answer questions 17-20.

Overall, we won the Little League championship game! Max hit a winning home run, and we all cheered as he rounded home plate. It was an astonishing win because the other team wins every year and we were down the whole game until the final inning. Our team hoisted the championship trophy up into the air and celebrated with joy. It was such a great game. After the game, my coach took my whole team to the diner and we got burgers, fries, and chocolate milkshakes. Max got grilled cheese because he is a vegetarian. This was the first championship game that our team has won in twenty years. My coach gave a speech while we were eating and said he was proud of our perseverance.

17. What is mostly likely the meaning of *astonishing* in the following sentence?

"It was an astonishing win because the other team wins every year and we were down the whole game until the final inning."

    a. Expected
    b. Surprising
    c. Celebrated
    d. Close

18. What is the main topic of the passage?
    a. A meal at the diner with his team
    b. A basketball team's victory
    c. Winning the baseball championship
    d. Vegetarian food options at a diner

19. Which of the following is the best description of the tone or mood of the passage?
    a. Excited
    b. Nervous
    c. Disappointed
    d. Informational

20. Which of the following can readers infer about Max?
    a. He is the narrator of the passage.
    b. He has been on the team for twenty years.
    c. He is overweight.
    d. He does not eat bacon.

Read the following passage, and then answer questions 21-24.

When renovating a home, there are several ways to save money. In order to keep a project cost effective, "Do It Yourself," otherwise known as "DIY," projects help put money back into the homeowner's pocket. For example, instead of hiring a contractor to do the demo, rent a dumpster and do the demolition. Another way to keep a home renovation cost effective is to compare prices for goods and services. Many contractors or distributors will match prices from competitors. Finally, if renovating a kitchen or bathroom, leave the layout of the plumbing and electrical the same. Once the process of moving pipes and wires is started, dollars start adding up. Overall, home renovations can be a pricey investment, but there are many ways to keep project costs down.

21. Which of the following statements is true based on the information in the passage?
    a. Home improvement projects can be expensive, but there are ways to keep costs down.
    b. Home renovations require a lot of work, which is why a contractor should be hired to complete the job.
    c. It is not necessary for homeowners to compare prices of contractors because they are their own best bet.
    d. Many contractors and distributors charge more than competitors for goods and services.

22. What is the meaning of the following sentence? "Do It Yourself," otherwise known as "DIY," projects help put money back into the homeowner's pocket.
    a. Homeowners get paid to do their own renovations.

b. Homeowners will find money in their house while they are doing repairs.

c. Hiring a contractor is more cost-effective than doing your own repairs.

d. Homeowners save money by doing home repairs themselves

23. Based on the opinion of the author, readers can infer that the author is likely which of the following?
    a. Someone who is a contractor
    b. Someone who is a distributer
    c. Someone who is very rich
    d. Someone who likes deals

24. Which of the following correctly lists the ways to keep renovation costs down, according to the author?
    a. Rent a dumpster, compare prices for goods and services, keep the layout of plumbing and electric.
    b. Rent a dumpster, compare prices for goods and services, change the pipes and wires.
    c. Hire a contractor for the demolition, compare prices for goods and services, keep the layout of plumbing and electric.
    d. Hire a contractor for the demolition, compare prices for goods and services, change the pipes and wires.

Read the following poem, and then answer questions 25-28.

Standing in front of the mirror, I like to look at my face

I smile and frown and laugh and scream, emotions all over the place

Sometimes I stand between my mom and dad, all three of us in a row

We look each other up and down from the tops of our heads to the tips of our toes

My mom says I have her nose and her ears and a smile just like my dad

Our shirts and pants look different though because I wear jeans and dad wears plaid

Our hair color is also different though, which is confusing to me

Dad has black, mom has blond, but mine is brown like the bark of a tree

My teacher told me we inherit genes from our parents that affect how we look and act

Some of our features look like one or both of them, while some are unique to us in fact.

I am glad that I carry parts of mom and dad on my face and in my heart

That way they are with me wherever I go, even when we are apart.

25. Which of the following pairs of words in the poem are homophones?
    a. Fact and act
    b. Genes and jeans
    c. Plaid and dad
    d. Mirror and inherit

26. Which of the following lines most likely was meant to have a figurative, not literal, meaning?
    a. My mom says I have her nose and her ears.
    b. We look each other up and down.
    c. My teacher told me we inherit genes from our parents that affect how we look and act.
    d. Standing in front of the mirror, I like to look at my face.

27. What does this poem teach readers?
    a. Children tend to look like people they are related to.
    b. If your hair color is brown, you don't look like your parents.
    c. Children and parents wear different types of pants.
    d. You should carry a mirror with you wherever you go.

28. Which of the following is likely not an inherited trait?
    a. Facial features
    b. Genes
    c. Jeans
    d. Behavior

Answer Explanations

1. A: Caribbean island destinations. The topic of the passage can be described in a one- or two-word phrase. Choices *B, C,* and *D* are all mentioned in the passage. However, they are too vague to be considered the main topic of the passage.

2. C: Family resorts and activities. Remember that supporting details help readers find out the main idea by answering questions like *who, what, where, when, why,* and *how.* In this question, cruises and local events are not talked about in the passage. However, family resorts and activities are talked about.

3. B: Opinion. An opinion is when the author states their own thoughts on a subject. In this sentence, the author says that the reader will not regret the vacation. The author says that it may be the best and most relaxing vacation. But this may not be true for the reader. Therefore, the statement is the author's opinion. Facts would have evidence, like that collected in a science experiment.

4. B: Persuade readers. The author is trying to persuade readers to go to a Caribbean island destination by giving the reader fun facts and a lot of fun options. Not only does the author give a lot of details to support their opinion, the author also implies that the reader would be "wrong" if they didn't want to visit a Caribbean island. This means the author is trying to persuade the reader to visit a Caribbean island.

5. D: Rain. Rain is the cause in this passage because it is why something happened. The effects are plants growing, rainbows, and puddle jumping.

6. A: Comparing. The author is comparing the plants, trees, and flowers. The author is showing how these things react the same to rain. They all get important nutrients from rain. If the author described the differences, then it would be contrasting, Choice *B.*

7. C: Necessary. *Vital* can mean different things depending on the context or how it is used. But in this sentence, the word *vital* means necessary. The word *vital* means full of life and energy. Choices *A* and *B, energetic* and *truthful,* do not make sense. Choice *D, dangerous,* is almost an antonym for the word we are looking for since the sentence says the nutrients are needed for growing. Something needed would not be dangerous. The best context clue is that it says the vital nutrients are needed, which tells us they are necessary.

8. C: Rainbows. This passage mentions several effects. Effects are the outcome of a certain cause. Remember that the cause here is rain, so Choice *A* is incorrect. Since the cause is rain, Choice *B*—brief spurts of sunshine—doesn't make sense because rain doesn't *cause* brief spurts of sunshine. Choice *C* makes the most sense because the effects of the rain in the passage are plants growing, rainbows, and puddle jumping. Lastly, Choice *D,* weather, is not an effect of rain but describes rain in a general sense.

9. A: Siberian huskies are great pets but require a lot of time and energy. In the passage, the writer talks about how huskies require lots of brushing and long walks and how they dig, making them not easy to care for. The author also talks about how friendly Siberian huskies can be, because they might greet a robber at their own house. This does not making them good guard dogs. Therefore, Siberian huskies are great pets but require a lot of time and energy.

10. C: Biased: The author may be biased because they show that they like one dog breed over another in an unfair way. Choice *A,* impartial, is the opposite of biased and means very fair, without being opinionated. Hasty, Choice *B*, means quick to judge, and irrational, Choice *D*, means something that doesn't make sense.

11. D: It is an experienced dog owner. We do not have any clues from the paragraph about if the narrator is a man or woman, so Choices *A* and *B* are incorrect. Also, the narrator talks about having other dogs before, so they cannot be a new dog owner. Choice *D* makes sense because the narrator talks about having other dogs before Lola, which means that they have been a dog owner before.

12. A: Choice *A* is a photo of a Siberian Husky like Lola. Test takers do not need to be familiar with different dog breeds to correctly answer this question. Instead, they can be detectives and use clues from the passage about what Lola looks like. For one, the narrator mentions Lola's long fur, which sounds bushy and full because it has to be brushed so much! Dogs in Choices *B* and *C* (the Chihuahua and the Dalmatian) are ruled out because of their short hair. The narrator also mentions that Lola has a "wolf-like appearance" that may scare a robber. Even though Choice *D* (a Shih-Tzu) has very long hair, that dog does not look like a wolf. Furthermore, Choices *B* and *C* do not look like wolves.

13. D: Readers should focus on the details in the passage to answer this question. The beginning of the passage, as well as the main idea, states that writing ten-minute plays may *seem* difficult, but it actually isn't. Therefore, Choice *A* is incorrect. Choices *B* and *D* are opposites. The passage mentions how descriptive details *are* important to help set the mood, tone, and theme, so Choice *B* is incorrect, and Choice *D* is the best answer. Lastly, it is said that the theme is set in the descriptive details. The theme should come right at the beginning of the play and not the climax, so Choice *C* is incorrect.

14. C: Pictures can tell stories as well, if not better, than words. This is a phrase used a lot in the English language. In the case of a short ten-minute play, playwrights would be smart to use images to cut down on the dialogue since ten minutes is not a long time. This passage was all about how writing a short play isn't actually that hard even for a new playwright. The author of the passage persuades readers by stating that pictures make it a lot simpler.

15. A: The protagonist of a story is the main character. Without knowing this, test takers can try to find the correct choice by using clues from the passage. The passage states: *As the play progresses, the protagonist must cross the point of no return in some way; this is the climax of the story. Then, as in a written story, you create a resolution to the life-changing event of the protagonist.* This information should help rule out Choices *C* and *D* (student and playwright) since it is clear that the protagonist is in the play. Choice *B*, actor, may be an attractive choice since an actor is in the play, but careful readers will notice that is says *the protagonist* meaning there is only one. There are likely multiple actors in the play, because the passage mentions dialogue, which must include at least two people.

16. B: The passage does not talk about how long a playwright spends doing revisions and rewrites. So, Choice *A* is incorrect. Choice *B* is correct because of the opening statement: "Learning how to write a ten-minute play may seem like a monumental task at first; but, if you follow a simple creative writing strategy, similar to writing a narrative story, you will be able to write a successful drama." None of the other choices are supported by points in the passage.

17. B: *Astonishing* most closely means surprising. Choice *A*, expected, can be ruled out because the same sentence mentions that the other team wins every year. Choice *D*, "a close win," does not make sense because the narrator does not say anything about the actual score. Readers may be tempted to choose *celebrated*, Choice *C*, because the passage mentions a lot of celebrating. However, using clues from the sentence that the other team always wins would help make *surprising* a better choice.

18. C: The passage talks about Little League and Max scoring the winning run. These are clues that it is about baseball. So, Choice *B* is incorrect. The main idea of the story is about the baseball team winning the championships. It is true that the team eats at the diner and one player is a vegetarian. However, these are supporting details.

19. A: This question was a little tricky because both *A* and *D* seem like they could be true. Nervous and disappointed, Choices *B* and *C*, should be easy to rule out because the narrator was happy about the win. The passage does mention that the other team usually wins, and it has been twenty years since the narrator's team won. However, these are just details. Choice *D*, informational, is not really a tone or mood. It refers to a type of writing that is educational. This passage is a story with excited emotion.

20. D: Readers are told that Max is a vegetarian. This means he does not eat meat. Bacon is a meat, so we can guess that Max does not eat bacon. Choice *A* is incorrect because the narrator mentions Max by name and doesn't say "I," so the narrator is not Max. We can also infer that Max has not been on the team for twenty years, because he would be too old! Readers may be tempted to choose Choice *C*, that Max is overweight, because it mentions that he follows a specific diet (vegetarian). However, he is active and in sports and got the winning run. Therefore, Choice *D* makes more sense than Choice *C*.

21. A: The main idea of the passage is that home improvement projects can be expensive. However, there are ways to keep the costs down. The details of the other choices go against what the passage says. So, they are incorrect. For example, the passage says that contractors will often price-match competitors. This makes Choice *D* incorrect. Choice *B* is incorrect because one of the author's main points is that they do not need to hire a contractor for all renovations. They can do it themselves as a DIY project. Choice *C* is incorrect because the passage does mention that some projects require professionals, but that comparing prices can minimize costs.

22. D: Something that is "like money on your pocket" means that it is money savings or a deal. This is a common phrase. Choice *A* doesn't make sense, because how would they get paid to do their own repairs? Who would pay them and why? Similarly, while some change may be found in couch cushions or loose money around some people's homes, Choice *B*, finding money while doing repairs, is not a likely choice. Choice *C* is incorrect based on the main idea and details mentioned in the passage. For example, readers are encouraged in the passage not to get a contractor to do the demolition, but to rent a dumpster themselves to save money.

23. D: Readers can guess that the author of the passage likes to find deals. For this reason, Choice *C* is more unlikely than Choice *D*, because if the narrator was very rich, they may be less interested in strategies to save money. The advice in the passage is mostly doing projects yourself, so the narrator is probably not a distributor or contractor. For this reason, Choices *C* and *D* are incorrect.

24. A: Readers must look carefully over the paragraph to find the author's advice. Readers will find that the author of the passage says to rent a dumpster, compare prices for goods and services, and keep the layout of plumbing and electric. The other answer choices had at least one incorrect suggestion.

25. B: Homophones are words that have the same pronunciation but different meanings or spellings. A good example of this is *new* and *knew*. New means something that has only existed for a short period of time. Knew, on the other hand, refers to the past tense of the verb to know, meaning to be aware of something. To answer this question correctly, test takers must be able to properly read the words genes and jeans. Genes are the genetic material that dictate a person's traits. Jeans are denim pants. The other answer choices provided were either pairs of rhyming words or simply two unrelated words.

26. A: My mom says I have her nose and her ears is an example of figurative language. Figurative language describes things using creative and imaginative terms, similes and metaphors, and poetic language. The words do not mean exactly what they say. In this case, the child narrating the poem does not truly have the mom's nose and ears. Those features are stuck on the mom's face! Instead, what is meant is that the child's features look very much like the nose and ears of the mom. This is a poetic expression. This is not a fact that should be taken with a literal meaning. The other choices are examples of lines in the poem with more literal meanings. Literal is when words mean what they say without any sort of imaginative language.

27. A: This poem teaches readers that children often have characteristics that look like their parents. This is because we inherit genes from our parents and these genes have something called DNA, which tells our body what we should look like. The other choices are not really lessons that the poem is teaching readers. Some children with brown hair look like their parents who may also have brown hair. Children and parents may wear different types of pants, but they don't have to. They can wear pants that are very similar. Lastly, it is not usually necessary to carry a mirror wherever one goes.

28. C: Genes are inherited, but jeans are clothing. Blue jeans may be passed down from an older sibling or parent as a hand-me-down. However, they are not a characteristic of an individual. Traits are what a person is as a whole.

Writing Sample

Test takers are given fifteen minutes to write a story about a picture that is provided. While this section is not scored, the writing sample is provided with the score report to each receiving school. This section gives test takers the opportunity to show their writing ability as well as show creativity and self-expression. Test takers should be sure that their stories have a beginning, a middle, and an end.

Planning should take place after looking at the picture or reading the prompt. This brainstorming stage is when writers consider their purpose and think of ideas that they can use in their writing. Drawing pictures like story webs are great tools to use during the planning stage. Drawing pictures can help connect the writing purpose to supporting details. They can also help begin the process of structuring the writing.

POWER Strategy for Writing

The POWER strategy helps all writers focus and do well during the writing process.

The POWER strategy stands for the following:

- Prewriting or Planning
- Organizing
- Writing a first draft
- Evaluating the writing
- Revising and rewriting

Prewriting and Planning
During the prewriting and planning phase, writers learn to think about their audience and purpose for the writing assignment. Then they gather information they wish to include in the writing. They do this from their background knowledge or new sources.

Organizing
Next, writers decide on the organization of their writing project. There are many types of organizational structures, but the common ones are: story/narrative, informative, opinion, persuasive, compare and contrast, explanatory, and problem/solution formats.

Writing
In this step, the writers write a first draft of their project.

Evaluating
In this stage, writers reread the writing and note the sections that are strong or that need improvement.

Revising and Rewriting
Finally, the writer incorporates any changes they wish to make based on what they've read. Then writers rewrite the piece into a final draft.

Elements of Effective Writing

The following are characteristics that make writing readable and effective:

- Ideas
- Organization
- Voice
- Word choice
- Sentence fluency
- Proper Writing Conventions
- Presentation

Ideas
This refers to the content of the writing. Writers should focus on the topic shown in the picture or prompt. They should narrow down and focus their idea, remembering that they only have fifteen minutes to plan and write! Then they learn to develop the idea and choose the details that best shows the idea to others.

Organization
Many writers are inclined to jump into their writing without a clear direction for where it is going. Organization helps plan out the writing so that it's successful. Your writing should have an introduction, a body, and a conclusion.

Introduction (beginning): Writers should invite the reader into their work with a good introduction. They should restate the prompt in their own words so that readers know what they are going to read about.

Body (middle): The body is where the main thoughts and ideas are put together. Thoughtful transitions between ideas and key points help keep readers interested. Writers should create logical and purposeful sequences of ideas.

Conclusion (end): Writers should include a powerful conclusion to their piece that summarizes the information but leaves the reader with something to think about.

Voice
Voice is how the writer uses words and how they use sentence structure to sound like themselves! It shows that the writing is meaningful and that the author cares about it. It is what makes the writing uniquely the author's own. It is how the reader begins to know the author and what they "sound like."

Word Choice
The right word choice helps the author connect with their audience. If the work is narrative, the words tell a story. If the work is descriptive, the words can almost make you taste, touch, and feel what you are reading! If the work is an opinion, the words give new ideas and invite thought. Writers should choose detailed vocabulary and language that is clear and lively.

Sentence Fluency
When sentences are built to fit together and move with one another to create writing that is easy to read aloud, the author has written with fluency. Sentences and paragraphs start and stop in just the right places so that the writing moves well. Sentences should have a lot of different of structures and lengths.

<u>Proper Writing Conventions</u>
Writers should make their writing clear and understandable through the use of proper grammar, spelling, capitalization, and punctuation.

<u>Presentation</u>
Writers should try to make their work inviting to the reader. Writers show they care about their writing when it is neat and readable.

Tips for the Writing Section

1. Don't panic! This section isn't scored. It is just a great way to show teachers how smart you are and how well you can tell a story and write. You can do it!

2. Use your time well. Fifteen minutes is quick! It is shorter than almost every TV show. Don't spend too much time doing any one thing. Try to brainstorm briefly and then get writing. Leave a few minutes to read it over and correct any spelling mistakes or confusing parts.

3. Be yourself! You are smart and interesting and teachers want to get to know you and your unique ideas. Don't feel pressured to use big vocabulary words if you aren't positive what they mean. You will be more understandable if you use the right word, not the fanciest word.

Practice Writing Sample

Tell a story using the picture below. Make sure that your story has a beginning, middle, and end.

FREE Test Taking Tips DVD Offer

To help us better serve you, we have developed a Test Taking Tips DVD that we would like to give you for FREE. **This DVD covers world-class test taking tips that you can use to be even more successful when you are taking your test.**

All that we ask is that you email us your feedback about your study guide. Please let us know what you thought about it – whether that is good, bad or indifferent.

To get your **FREE Test Taking Tips DVD**, email freedvd@studyguideteam.com with "FREE DVD" in the subject line and the following information in the body of the email:

   a. The title of your study guide.

   b. Your product rating on a scale of 1-5, with 5 being the highest rating.

   c. Your feedback about the study guide. What did you think of it?

   d. Your full name and shipping address to send your free DVD.

If you have any questions or concerns, please don't hesitate to contact us at freedvd@studyguideteam.com.

Thanks again!

71640318R00049

Made in the USA
Middletown, DE
27 April 2018